Bread Salt & PLUM BRANDY

A True Story of Love and Adventure
in a Foreign Land

Lisa Fisher Cazacu and Rosemary Colgrove

Aventine Press

This is a true story. However, some names have been changed to protect persons and organizations that do not want their identity revealed, or their privacy compromised.

Grateful appreciation is extended to the following for permission to reprint previously published material:
- Jerry Morton (*Romania*, Jerry Lee Press, 1996)
- Andrei Cordescu (*The Hole in the Flag: A Romanian Exile's Story of Return and Revolution*, William Morrow and Company, 1991; Copyright 1991 by Andrei Codrescu.) Reprinted with permission of The Lazear Agency.
- Telegraph.co.uk (www.telegraph.co.uk/news/worldnews/europe/romania/1497142, *British diplomat extends helping hand to Europe's last leper colony*, Michael Leidig, August 27, 2005).

Front and back cover designs by Melinda Wing.

Back cover photograph courtesy of the *Williamson County Sun*.

Lisa's Georgetown wedding photo courtesy of Brendan Bannon.

Published by Aventine Press
750 State St. #319
San Diego CA, 92101
Library of Congress Control Number: 2009924678
Library of Congress Cataloging-in-Publication Data

ISBN: 1-59330-579-6

Printed in the United States of America.

For the Romanian people, who touched my heart and changed my life.

For the United States of America, which gave me the chance to experience this remarkable adventure.

Finally, for my *urs,* my partner, my husband, Andrei. You make my life complete, and a constant whirlwind of excitement.

— Lisa

For Dean, whose patience and support (fortified by plenty of *tuica*) allowed me to complete this project.

— Rosemary

CONTENTS

Preface   1
Prologue   3

1   What Was I Thinking?   13
2   Goodbye to Margaritas and BBQ   21
3   Ploiesti: Arrival in an Alien Land   25
4   Life with My *Gazda*   29
5   Boot Camp   33
6   Superstitions, Gypsies, and Orphans   39
7   The Funeral   45
8   Giurgiu   49
9   The Mission Begins   57
10 Failure to Launch (First Assignment)   63
11 Finding My Groove   67
12 Bills, Bras, and Barnyard Animals   77
13 Slobozia, Timisoara, and Baia Mare   83
14 Horseradish Is a Root   89
15 You Can't Get There from Here   95
16 Rain Showers and Champagne Toasts   109
17 Madame Director   115
18 'Twas the Night Before Christmas and the Pigs Were Nervous 121
19 Carpe Every Diem   127
20 Legal Aid   135
21 Growing Up in the Shadow of Ceausescu   141
22 The Tourists   155
23 Summer Highs   163
24 Faith, Hope, Not So Much Charity   169
25 Hearts, Diamonds, and Visas   175
26 Julia's Wedding   181
27 Joy to the World   185
28 Sex in the City   191
29 A Wedding and a Medical Emergency   197
30 Repatriation and Americanization   203
31 Wedding Bells — Again   207

Epilogue   209
The Peace Corps Today   213
Acknowledgments   215
Author Biographies   216

PREFACE

In spite of centuries of invasion, oppression, and unspeakable brutality, the Romanian people are some of the most generous on the planet, welcoming you into their homes and hearts with the traditional offering of bread, salt, and *tuica,* a potent, homemade plum brandy.

Often considered the most beautiful country in Eastern Europe, Romania's rich cultural heritage still flourishes, little changed since the Middle Ages. In rural areas, peasants still plow their fields with horses and harvest their crops with hand-made wooden tools in a time-honored pastoral cycle. Life is celebrated with passion, pomp, and the joyous folk music that is so uniquely Romanian.

When I came to Romania in 2002 as a Peace Corps Volunteer, the country was still reeling from decades of repressive communist rule. Since then, the country has made significant progress in its difficult and painful transition to democracy and a free market economy. Toward that end, Romania has been a member of the North Atlantic Treaty Organization since 2004, and was accepted into the European Union in January 2007.

Romania would test my resolve and touch my soul in ways I never imagined, and in the end, I gained much more than I gave. I will always be grateful to the Romanian people for allowing me to come into their homes and hearts for two memorable years.

But this is more than a story of humanitarian service. It is also the story of Andrei, a young lawyer from Bucharest, who experienced first-hand the horrors of Nicolae Ceausescu's reign of terror. Andrei would ultimately change my life.

Finally, I apologize to the people of Romania if I have touched on sensitive or negative subjects. I did so in good faith, hoping that such revelations will serve to increase insight and awareness of the issues.

Lisa Fisher Cazacu
Georgetown, Texas
April 2009

PROLOGUE

The Rape of Romania
A Historical Perspective

It is impossible to understand my story without knowing something of the incredible struggle the Romanian people endured for 45 years, under a brutal and tyrannical communist regime. This perspective is offered as an overview of that dark period, which lasted from 1945 until the bloody revolution of 1989 ended Romania's long nightmare.

> *"The Romans were here nearly 2,000 years ago, followed over the centuries by Magyars, Turks, Austrians, and Romanians, among others, all leaving cultural reminders of their own.... But of all the changes that have occurred in this small East European country, few were as shattering as the revolution of 1989 when — if only via television — the whole world came to Romania."*

> — Jerry Morton, author, *Romania*

The calm before the storm

From the end of World War II until the fall of Communism in 1989, much of Romania's history — indeed anything Romanian — was kept under wraps, totally isolated from the Western world by a regime of terror, intimidation, and oppression. About the only thing that survived was the amazing spirit of the Romanian people, who are finally tasting freedom and a measure of prosperity, something they have long been denied and for which they paid a terrible price.

Before world wars and the ravages of communism obliterated Romania from Western consciousness, the country had been innovative and progressive, even prosperous. Few people know that Romania produced some of the world's first oil; in 1857, the first oil wells in the Eastern Hemisphere were drilled in Ploiesti, Romania. In 1856,

Romania's capital, Bucharest, became the first city in the world to be illuminated by oil lamps and, in 1884, Timisoara became the first European city with electric street lights.

Romania enjoyed its most prosperous, democratic, and happiest time in modern history during the period between the two World Wars. There was universal suffrage, and a new Constitution — one of the most democratic in Europe — was adopted in 1923. In 1937, Romania produced 7.2 million tons of oil, making it the second largest petroleum producer in Europe and seventh in the world. Economic development flourished.

But the tragic consequences of World War II and the resulting communist occupation would change things in ways no one could have ever imagined.

The shadows lengthen

In 1947, King Mihai I was deposed and Romania became a Communist People's Republic, under the control of Soviet Russia. Industries were nationalized, and the economy was restructured. A harsh totalitarian government came into power, based on the surveillance and repression of Romanian citizens. Totally isolated from the rest of the world, Romania was plunged into a black hole of despair, which would last for almost 50 years.

In an attempt to eliminate opponents of the new regime, up to two million people were imprisoned for vague political or economic reasons, most of them without a trial. Thousands of Romanians died in prisons, and thousands more suffered horrific abuses for their crimes, real or imagined. More than 100,000 people were worked to death on the Danube-Black Sea Canal, or were simply shot.

One of the first problems facing the new regime was how to feed the growing urban population. In 1949, the government initiated an agricultural collectivization program, hoping to stimulate domestic food production. Under this program, the state simply seized the peasants' land and forced them onto cooperative farms. To expedite things, paranoid government agents roamed the countryside, arresting thousands of peasants for the crime of being "class enemies," or private farmers. Many centuries-old villages were torched or bulldozed into oblivion, along with a priceless heritage.

The plan was cruel and totally ineffective. Severe food shortages resulted, so by late 1951, the government was forced to revise its policy, permitting the farmers to keep their land but give up the bulk of their harvest to the state.

Meanwhile, the ubiquitous and dreaded secret police, or Securitate — with its enormous system of spies and informers — swiftly suppressed all opposition. Surveillance, intimidation, and torture were the currency of the regime. Mail was intercepted, contact with foreigners banned, phones bugged, and ordinary citizens placed under secret surveillance. Those who were suspected of disloyalty to the State were arrested, imprisoned, tortured or murdered. Informers reported on guests in people's homes, where people went, and with whom they talked. Friends, lovers, families — even young children — were compelled to spy on each other's personal lives. Radios were silent because the citizens were well aware of the penalty for listening to a forbidden station.

Spying became a condition of survival, deception a way of life. People were forced to make impossible compromises, choosing their betrayals carefully, often in the hope of securing jobs or gaining better treatment for imprisoned friends or relatives. Ultimately, thousands of families were separated forever by a simple signature on a false warrant.

Fear was a palpable and deadly motivator.

To spy on Romania's 22 million people, the Securitate relied on about 14,000 official agents, plus another 600,000 or so "voluntary" informants recruited from among the nation's citizens. (Reference: Cold War International History Project.) Some informants were threatened or blackmailed into collaborating, others volunteered their services out of fear or misguided patriotism. Many survived by offering worthless information to protect their jobs without compromising family or friends.

In 2005, sixteen years after the revolution, the Securitate archives were opened to the public in an attempt to mend the lingering wounds of the Romanian people (and perhaps to score points toward securing admission to the European Union). The files revealed a paranoid government that inspired fear and distrust in its citizens and set friends and families against each other. Among the documents contained in the archives were thousands of transcriptions of secretly taped phone conversations, detailed reports of people under surveillance, even copies of private correspondence.

To the Romanian citizens — miserable, hungry, and demoralized — it seemed things couldn't get worse. But in March 1965, Nicolae Ceausescu, an egomaniacal high-school dropout, came to power. His extreme policies of intimidation, deprivation, and brutality would ultimately destroy much of Romania's culture, bankrupt its economy, and impoverish the people. Romania would not see the light of liberty for another 24 years.

The dictatorship of Nicolae Ceausescu was one of the most evil and corrupt regimes in 20th-century Europe. Most historians believe Ceausescu was probably a mental case of extreme pathological dimensions, but this does little to mitigate the tragic effects of his evil ambition. Under Ceausescu, the state would control every facet of the lives of its citizens, how many children a woman could have, how many light bulbs you could use in your home, how much heat you could use, and how much food you could eat.

By 1971, Ceausescu's paranoia was in full bloom. Free speech was severely limited, and the media firmly under the iron grip of the state. It was even forbidden to own a typewriter without proper registration, and, once registered, a state official would personally visit your home or business and tell you exactly where to place the machine.

The baby police

Convinced that the key to industrial expansion was to grow the labor force, Ceausescu tried to control procreation, banning abortions and contraception for all married woman under the age of 40 who had fewer than four children.

> *"The fetus is the property of the entire society. Anyone who avoids having children is a deserter who abandons the laws of national continuity."*

> — Nicolae Ceausescu, 1966

Under his new policy, all married women were required to produce four children or be penalized by "celibacy" taxes, often as much as 10 to 20 percent of their monthly wages. Single adults as well as married couples with no children were also subject to the higher taxes.

To enforce compliance with his bizarre mandate, Ceausescu brought in the "baby police" to ensure that women were fulfilling their partisan duty. Women were routinely rounded up at work and brought to clinics for humiliating medical examinations. Accordingly, women gave birth to children they could not afford to raise, and unwanted pregnancies and back-street abortions (available for as little as a carton of cigarettes) increased dramatically. Thousands of orphaned, abandoned, or disabled children were sent away to miserable state institutions, where there was not enough food, medicine, clothing, or staff to care for them. Desperate women helplessly surrendered their children to the State in the mistaken hope that they would be properly cared for.

To house the "surplus" children, Ceausescu created severely under-staffed orphanages, designed to produce citizens with no loyalty to anyone or anything except the regime. If they survived at all, the children grew up in an environment totally devoid of any mental or physical stimulation or caring human contact. Workers in the orphanages dealt with their overwhelming workload by keeping the smaller children in their cribs 24 hours a day. Lying two and three to a bed, the babies received little attention from the desensitized and beleaguered staff.

After the fall of Ceausescu in 1989, thousands of starving, neglected children were found living in these wretched institutions, which most Romanians never knew existed. The Western press reported rooms filled with silent children. Nobody came if they cried, so they didn't cry anymore. And in the institutions that had basements, there were children who hadn't seen daylight for years.

The politics of duplicity

In the 1980s, Ceausescu introduced a new sort of social engineering, designed to resettle Romania's rural population into urban apartment blocks. This would result in a more concentrated labor force while providing additional land for agricultural development. A more insidious but unpublished goal of the policy was to increase the state's ability to maintain control over its citizens. With people scattered all over the place, it was difficult to keep an eye on things. By forcibly relocating more than 11 million peasants to grim, urban apartment blocs with communal kitchens and resident managers (informers), the peasants could be converted from farmers to factory laborers, all under the vigilant eye of the state.

The program was haphazardly implemented and ultimately abandoned, but not before Ceausescu had destroyed over seven thousand rural villages.

Human rights abuses continued to escalate during the 1980s. The Securitate stepped up its efforts to eliminate dissent through such tactics as framed accusations, public humiliation, and tighter censorship — all designed to intimidate and repress people, and to extract information. Opposition to authority was not a part of the Romanian psyche.

With a collapsing economy and a rising national debt (approximately $10.2 billion by end of 1981), Ceausescu adopted a severe austerity program in which Romania would pay back its entire foreign debt by choking domestic consumption and exporting all of its food. Ceausescu did, in fact, succeed in paying off the debt — at a devastating cost. Food, electricity, heat, and gasoline were strictly rationed, and harsh penalties were imposed for hoarding. Most of the country's available food was exported, and starving citizens queued in long lines for the meager leftovers.

To conserve energy, offices and public places had to be kept no warmer than 16° C (63 ° F) in winter, hot water was severely restricted (only one day a week in some areas), and people could use only a single 40-watt bulb to light their homes. Families were allowed only four pounds of meat per year, and dairy products were extremely scarce. By the mid 1980s, meat was no longer available and monthly food rations in some areas were reduced to about two pounds of sugar, two pounds of flour, five eggs, and 18 ounces of margarine.

During the winter of 1984-85, Bucharest was gripped by devastating cold. The streets were dark and silent, automobile traffic was banned, and heat and hot water turned off. Hospitals were ordered to shut off incubators and life support systems, and in the sub-zero temperatures, many perished needlessly.

While the Romanian people stoically endured the harsh conditions, despair enveloped the country. Cold, starving, and in the dark, their misery was utter and without hope. Meanwhile, Ceausescu and his family dined on golden plates in their splendid (and heated) palaces, choosing from an array of imported entrees each evening.

Final assault

Over the years, Ceausescu had created a massive personality cult, and his biggest and most beloved fan was himself. His image appeared everywhere, in every city, in every village, on posters and on buildings. In the mid-1980s, Ceausescu began his final assault, which would put his mark irrevocably on Bucharest. Dictatorship had its perks. You didn't really need permission to destroy a country.

A man of immense narcissistic ambition, Ceausescu wanted Bucharest to be a monument to the grandeur and importance of his regime. He would ultimately obliterate much of the historic center of Bucharest to make room for the Centru Civic with its massive and grandiose "Palace of the People," reportedly the third-largest building on the planet after the Pentagon and the Tibetan Potala. Today the massive monument to tyranny dominates central Bucharest and is home to the Romanian Parliament and the National Museum of Contemporary Art.

During the "reconstruction," nearly four square miles of the city center were razed, including some of the city's oldest and most beautiful buildings. Historic churches and synagogues, schools, a hospital, and more than 9,000 homes — many of which had stood for hundreds of years — simply disappeared. ·

Ceausescu was never really fond of individual houses, which were much more difficult to spy upon. By destroying them and relocating the displaced citizens into concentrated apartment units, surveillance would be infinitely simpler — and unavoidable. Thus, more than 40 thousand inhabitants were ultimately resettled into dreary concrete apartment blocs on the outskirts of the city, where up to ten families often shared a single kitchen.

Escape from tyranny

The end of Romania's long nightmare finally came in December 1989. On the morning of December 22, Nicolae Ceausescu made his final appeal from the balcony of the Central Committee headquarters. The situation was now out of his control, and his army was reportedly joining the insurgents. Shouted down by a militant crowd no longer afraid of reprisal, the aging dictator and his wife fled the capital by helicopter, never to return.

Justice for Romania's first couple was swift and final. On Christmas Day, barely hours after their capture, Nicolae and Elena Ceausescu were brought before a hastily convened military tribunal and sentenced to death by firing squad.

For the first time in four decades, Christmas Day was declared a national holiday. Citizens joyfully celebrated both the birth of Christ as well as the death of a brutal dictator.

Accusing Ceausescu of "acts incompatible with human dignity" and "destroying the people whose leaders they claimed to be," the bill of indictment included genocide, armed attack on the people and the state, destruction of buildings and state institutions, and undermining the national economy.

During the trial of Nicolae and Elena Ceausescu, held at Tirgoviste Military Base, General Gica Popa, the chief prosecutor, said:

> *"It is very difficult for us to act, to pass a verdict on people who even now do not want to admit to the criminal offenses that they have committed during 25 years and ... to the genocide, not only in Timisoara and Bucharest, but primarily also to the criminal offenses committed during the past 25 years . . . They not only deprived the people of heating, electricity, and foodstuffs, they also tyrannized the soul of the Romanian people. They not only killed children, young people and adults in Timisoara and Bucharest, they allowed Securitate members to wear military uniforms to create the impression among the people that the army is against them. They wanted to separate the people from the army. They used to fetch people from orphans' homes . . . whom they trained in special institutions to become murderers of their own people. You were so impertinent as to cut off oxygen lines in hospitals and to shoot people in their hospital beds. The Securitate had hidden food reserves on which Bucharest could have survived for months, the whole of Bucharest."*

* Transcript of the trial of Nicolae and Elena Ceausecu, as shown on Romanian and Austrian television. www.ceausescu. org

After the trial, the deposed 71-year-old tyrant reportedly shuffled from the courtroom singing the *Internationale* (a socialist hymn) and proclaiming that history would vindicate him. Shortly thereafter, Ceausescu and his wife were shot dead in a shabby, snow-covered courtyard.

1
What Was I Thinking?

Baia Mare, Romania, August 2002

I was an American woman traveling alone. It would never have happened to a Romanian. And unless I was missing something about Romanian train practices, I was pretty sure a 'massage' was not included in the ticket price. Horrified, I realized I was the only passenger in the entire train car. Whatever I tried to do, he could overpower me.

—From Lisa Fisher's journal

In August 2002, I was one year and six months into my two-year Peace Corps service in post-communist Romania. By then, I had already experienced a lifetime of exhilaration and frustration as an American volunteer serving in a foreign land. I had encountered blizzards, stifling heat, wretched poverty, neglected orphans, and bureaucratic nightmares, but I had also met endearing souls, courageous people, and little angels. The remarkable spirit of the Romanian people as they struggled to adapt to their newfound freedom was truly inspiring, and I was more determined than ever to finish what I had set out to do.

Yet things would get worse before they got better, and in the end, the Peace Corps would prove to be the most challenging, most rewarding personal journey of my life. It would, as the Peace Corps says, be the toughest job I would ever love.

But to understand my journey, you must first understand how I arrived at this place and time.

* * *

In November 2001, my life changed in ways I could never have imagined. I was invited to join the United States Peace Corps. When the official letter of invitation, printed in Times Roman on Peace Corps letterhead, finally arrived, I was afraid to open it, suspecting that I was about to make the most foolish decision of my life.

Anxiously, I read the assignment description:

> *Accommodations, food availability, entertainment, and working conditions will vary. Heat and water may be available only during certain hours of the day, and in some localities hot water is rarely available. Winters in Romania are cold while summers may be hot. Air conditioning and reliable heating are normally not available.*

I have always thrived in situations that require me to step outside my comfort zone and explore new ideas and surroundings. But I had no idea how far outside of the comfortable and familiar I would be stepping. I knew nothing about Romania, and I had no idea how deeply I would be drawn into this fascinating, frustrating, remarkable place.

My journey to Romania really began in March 2001. At that time, I was quite happy with my life in Georgetown, Texas. I had wonderful friends, I traveled for work and pleasure, I lived in the perfect apartment, and nearby Austin was my playground. Then I learned that the company I worked for was downsizing, and my job would be eliminated.

I had been laid off before. Twice. The first two times I was working for under-funded non-profits. This time the national economy got in the way. The fact that I truly loved my job in public relations made my impending termination all the more difficult. My co-workers were talented and wonderful, and the work was challenging. I looked forward to going to work every day and I was devastated that something I cared so much about was going away. And this time, the idea of yet another career-motivated job search did not inspire.

The day I found out that I had lost my job, I went home and took stock of my life. I was young, single, resourceful, and independent. I liked people and people seemed to like me. I had no kids, no dog, no mortgage (and no trust fund). I needed a plan.

I scoured the Internet searching for an opportunity that might lead to adventure and fulfillment. Eventually I found my way to the Peace Corps Web site. The more I read, the more excited I became. Here were new challenges, new environments, and new opportunities to serve. I felt like the words on the screen had been written just for me. I had always been interested in other cultures and I enjoyed helping people — this just might be my "it" job, my chance to expand my horizons and do something that wasn't just for me. I didn't think about the fact that the Peace Corps gets thousands of applications every year, and that only about one in four is accepted.

The prospect of Peace Corps service wasn't entirely a stretch. All my life I had challenged myself. Whether it was a triathlon, an Outward Bound adventure, or a new job, I liked to be completely prepared — mentally, emotionally, and physically. I hoped this same approach would help me to become a Peace Corps Volunteer.

* * *

The Peace Corps application process turned out to be labor-intensive, frustrating, and really, really long. The online application presented a broad range of questions, among them my geographical preferences. I checked Europe/Asia. Asked if there was any place I would not go, I checked Africa. I knew that I could not survive in a very remote area, or anyplace where I had to haul my own water. It wasn't that I was naïve, lazy, or selfish. I was simply facing facts. I knew that I did not have the coping skills that would be required in a third-world country. Although there were many urban assignments in Africa, I thought that Europe or Asia would give me the best chance of success. And even though I could not commit to the seriously difficult hardships of some Peace Corp assignments, I hoped that I could do work that would matter.

It took me a week to finish the application, which included numerous essays, as well as detailed personal and medical information. When I finally hit SEND, I thought, "Here I go!" Actually it was more like,

"What have I done?"

After the Peace Corps processed my initial application, they asked for additional information. *(Was this a good sign?)* I had to submit an Aspiration Statement, a Motivation Statement, an extensive medical history, and three letters of reference. I also had to undergo complete medical and dental physicals, get fingerprinted, and pass a background check.

The next step was a one-on-one interview with a Peace Corps recruiter, a personal evaluation process designed to assess my suitability for service, as well as my cultural sensitivity, skill levels, commitment, and possible obstacles to my being an effective volunteer.

I had my interview in late August at the University of Texas in Austin. I prepared for this meeting as if it was a job interview, but the questions would be much more personal. The screening procedure is designed to allow the Peace Corps to "discover" your character, sort of like peeling back the layers of an onion. In an intense two-hour session, we discussed everything from my background, education, personal habits, and coping skills to my motivation, expectations, and the challenges of living an ocean apart (and then some) from all that was familiar.

At the end of the meeting, the recruiter told me he was recommending me for service in an environmental program as an A-match (almost match), probably because of some work I had done in environmental public relations. That was a long shot perhaps, but the Peace Corps needed environmentalists. I was assigned to a program in Eastern Europe that was scheduled to begin in the spring, but I would not find out exactly where I was going for several months.

I was in! Well, almost. I still needed to get medical clearance. And my medical history would nearly keep me out of the Peace Corps.

I was living in central Texas, which has to be the allergy capital of the world. Like millions of other Texans, I got weekly allergy shots for local pollens.

In September, I received a letter from the Peace Corps, but my excitement was quickly dispelled when I read it. "We have reviewed your medical records and determined that we must defer our evaluation of your medical qualification until you have completed your allergy immunotherapy."

Basically, I would have to wait two years and complete my allergy shots before reapplying. Apparently my doctor had noted on the medical form that I was to receive the injections for a period of two years.

A few minutes later, I was on the phone, pleading with the nurse at the allergy clinic. "You've got to talk to the doctor. Please tell her if she doesn't write 'while living in Central Texas' on my medical form, she is going to totally screw up my life." Without those five words, I might as well kiss my Peace Corps prospects good-bye. Happily, my doctor complied. A few weeks later, I was cleared. At least for my allergies.

The second obstacle I faced was that I was seeing a therapist because of an incident I had experienced on New Year's Eve of the previous year. It happened in New Orleans on Bourbon Street in a crowd so tightly packed I could not even lift my arms. I was, quite literally, immobilized. In utter panic, I forced myself through the crowd, escaping over a fence and down a side street. For the rest of the trip, I refused to be in any situation involving a crowd. In New Orleans on New Year's Eve, this is pretty much impossible so I spent a lot of time in the hotel.

Once back home, I decided my behavior was possibly a bit irrational and sought counseling, ultimately realizing that it was the loss of personal control that had contributed to my behavior in New Orleans.

On October 25, I received a second letter from the Peace Corps. "We are deferring your medical clearance until you complete your therapy. We ask that you wait for a period of two years following the completion of your therapy before you continue pursuing Peace Corps service."

I had been derailed by a single anxiety attack.

In retrospect, the fact that I had actually sought therapy for the incident was the right thing to do. Vanity notwithstanding, I quickly decided there was no way I was going to let an anxiety attack keep me out of the Peace Corps. I immediately called my Peace Corps medical screener and explained my situation. Rob had heard a lot of "situations." Mine was probably not unique, but almost certainly I was the most persistent (annoying). We spoke every day and soon became fast friends, sharing a common interest in museums, theater, and movies. We even shared the same birthday. Rob became my advocate and understood that my counseling was a positive thing. He eventually got me cleared on this issue, although my acceptance would not become official until I received my letter of invitation.

Weeks passed and I received no official letter. It was already early November and the anticipation was exhausting (there is only so much cleaning one can do). Should I move out of my apartment? Should I have really sold all that stuff at the garage sale?

Anxious to find out *where* I would be spending my two years of Peace Corps service, I tracked down my placement officer and called her up. By now, Lisa Fisher had become a household word at Peace Corps headquarters.

"On November 17, I'm having a party to celebrate my fortieth birthday, and it would be really great if I could tell my friends *where* I'm going," I whined. The Peace Corps' tolerance for whining was apparently infinite.

"OK, this is what I'll do," my placement officer said. "The official letter inviting you to join Peace Corps will be going out soon, so I'll go ahead and tell you now. You are going to Romania."

There it was: five little words that would forever change my life.

Romania. The word rolled off my tongue like I had a clue. But where exactly was Romania? I had no idea, other than it was somewhere in Eastern Europe. Besides the obvious associations — Transylvania, Dracula, orphans, Nadia Comaneci — I knew embarrassingly little about the country. I was aware that Romania was a former communist country, and I was vaguely familiar with the name of Romanian dictator Nicolae Ceausescu, but beyond that, I was a blank slate.

I would soon, however, become much better informed.

On December 17, I finally received my letter of invitation, as well as my assignment description, a language pamphlet, housing questionnaire, and a welcome packet. I also received e-mail contact information for volunteers already serving in Romania, which would prove invaluable.

I had been assigned to the Environmental Management and Education program and was scheduled to leave for orientation in Washington, D.C. on February 13. We would depart for Romania the following day.

Eagerly, I studied the project backgrounder:

Romania is experiencing one of the most significant economic, political, and social transformations in its history. After more than 40 years under communism, the country has established a parliamentary democracy, opened a free press, and is moving toward a free market economy. The courage, struggles, and optimism of the Romanian people to establish new economic, legal, and social systems have captured the world's attention . . .

In response to a request from the Romanian government, the Peace Corps had created the environmental program to assist local organizations in coping with the challenges caused by years of environmental neglect and abuse during the former communist regime. The Peace Corps promised to match my skills with an organization where I would have "a good opportunity to make a difference in the lives of Romanians." As a volunteer, it would be essential to offer my skills in the spirit of sharing, in working *with* instead of *for*. My projects would not be sustainable if the Romanians could not continue the work after I left. Flexibility would be very important. If I were not flexible, I would fail. The F word would become my Peace Corps mantra.

Suddenly, I was having titanic reservations. I kept waking up in the middle of the night, wavering between certain uncertainty and profound anxiety. I worried about whether I would be effective, if the people would like me, if I would be able to survive in a totally alien place. What if this really was an incredibly stupid idea?

But there was no turning back now, and so I began preparing for my journey. I attacked the packing list first. I had been e-mailing some of the volunteers already in Romania and one of the best pieces of advice I received was to bring a good pair of snow boots. I spent $125 on a pair of comfortable Lowa hiking boots that I ended up wearing almost every day from November until March. Other recommendations included Ziploc bags, favorite spices, bath-size towels, duct tape, flashlight, batteries, and clothespins. Except for the duct tape and snow boots, I might have been packing for summer camp.

Next I started packing up my apartment. Unwilling to pay $3,000 for two-and-a-half years of storage, I worked out an arrangement with a local storage company. My pitch went something like this: "I'm going to be serving in the Peace Corps and while I'm gone, I'll be maintaining a Web site and the local newspaper will be publishing my journals. I'll mention you in a column and put your company link on my Web site if you'll provide free storage for my stuff while I'm gone."

I was ecstatic when the storage company agreed to the trade-off, even upgrading me to a larger unit when the smaller size wasn't sufficient. My friends were also extremely generous: one of them created a Web site for me, someone else drafted my will and power of attorney, and another bought my car for exactly what I owed on it.

The last step was the biggest challenge: How to fit two years' worth of stuff into the recommended two suitcases and a backpack? I was, after all, the gal with more than a hundred pairs of shoes. Somehow, I would have to find room for all my clothes (four seasons' worth), my favorite foods, computer equipment, incidentals, cosmetics, books, footgear, CDs, DVDs, and cherished mementos. And my checked luggage could not exceed 140 pounds, with a maximum weight allowance of 70 pounds per bag. So I bought a duffle bag. Then, on a whim, I called the Peace Corps desk officer for Romania. "Hi David, this is Lisa Fisher. I want to talk to you about this luggage thing ..."

David explained that this was not a Peace Corps rule, but rather an airline regulation. My mind was spinning. "If I can get three bags on the airline, then it doesn't matter to the Peace Corps?" Although he assured me that it wouldn't, he added, "Keep in mind that you're responsible for hauling your own luggage."

No problem, I thought. If it meant getting to take everything I needed, hauling it would be a piece of cake.

"So," I continued, "if I show up with three bags, will I be the person with the most luggage?" He told me that someone had once showed up with five pieces of luggage. (Looking back now at everything I hauled across the ocean — what was I *thinking*?)

I did, in fact, end up with more luggage than anyone else. And I would be harassed for two years by fellow volunteers about having the most stuff. But those same volunteers would happily share a lot of that stuff!

2
Goodbye to Margaritas and BBQ

Georgetown, Texas, February 10, 2002
For months, my departure has seemed surreal and distant.
Now that everything is imminent, I am suddenly overcome
with all kinds of free-flying emotions. The excitement about
what lies ahead is undeniable, but I am also filled with sadness
about leaving my family and friends. I will miss margaritas,
sushi, and BBQ, but I know I will be gaining so much more.
Not being able to call Julia ten times a day will be hard, but
through creativity, my digital camera, and the Internet, I will
find new ways to share my new experiences.

The day before I was scheduled to leave, I woke up feeling like I had swallowed a sword. I had strep throat. All the last-minute details I needed to take care of and the dinner I had planned with friends and family were suddenly replaced with pain, fever, and misery. Late in the afternoon, I went to the doctor and got some antibiotics, then went to bed to sleep it off. When the alarm went off at 4:00 a.m. the next morning, I wasn't at all sure I was going anywhere, much less on a transcontinental journey to Romania.

I arrived at the Austin airport very early on February 13th, feeling eager, miserable, scared, and exhilarated. Airport security was still on high alert; it had only been five months since the attacks of 9/11. At the check-in counter, I had to pay $80 in excess-weight charges for my third suitcase (a bargain considering all the life-supporting essentials it contained, right?).

My good friend Chris and best friend, Julia, came to see me off. It was like a scene from a bad movie, with tears flowing nonstop. I suddenly realized that I was — most profoundly — leaving. I was about to begin a voyage of more than 6,000 miles, with a single step, a large bottle of aspirin, and three overstuffed suitcases.

My destination was Washington, DC, but I would have to change flights in Atlanta. In Atlanta, I headed straight to the bathroom where I spent my time hugging the porcelain throne. I hoped to remain there until all the nausea and heartache had passed, but my flight was called all too soon.

As we approached Reagan National Airport, there was an obvious increase in security precautions. We were told several times that if anyone stood up or moved from their seats, the plane would be diverted. It was both scary and totally understandable in this new post-9/11 world. But we landed without incident and on schedule.

I took a shuttle to the hotel, where I met up with 39 other Peace Corps Trainees (PCTs) who were also going to Romania. I had packed, according to PC instructions, enough clothes for the first four days in my backpack, so I locked the rest of my luggage in a closet in the hotel lobby. Hauling my luggage was a pain. In the end, I would be happy I had over packed, right? I wasn't.

My hotel roommate was a cheery, petite thirty-something social worker from Georgetown, Kentucky. Lourrae and I would end up serving in the same Romanian town.

There was barely time to freshen up before orientation began. As soon as I entered the conference room, I spotted David, my Peace Corps contact during the admission process. I told him I had strep throat.

"I'm going to pretend you didn't tell me that," he said, "because if you told me, I could not allow you get on the plane tomorrow. However, when you get to Bucharest and meet the doctor, please tell him immediately that you have strep." I promised to do as I was told.

Once the socializing began, I immediately forgot how bad I felt. I was instantly attracted to the youngest guy in the group, a gregarious 22-year-old intellectual named Peter Brown, who would become a good friend during my service in Romania. I partnered with Peter in a game called My New Best Friend, in which you shared what unusual item you were bringing to Romania. One PCT was bringing a meat clever. I hoped it was for culinary purposes. Other items destined for service in Romania were a Travel Twister game, hair dye, and a lifetime supply of home perm.

There were 40 of us in Group 14, so called because we were the 14th Peace Corps group to serve in Romania. Twenty of us would serve as volunteers in the social program, and another twenty (including me) would serve in the environmental program. Our group included a retired Wall Street broker, several lawyers, an immunologist, students, social workers, engineers, nonprofit administrators, even a cruise director. There was one married couple. Eight volunteers were older than 50; two were in their 40s, nine in their 30s, and the rest were twenty-somethings. There was an equal mix of men and women.

What we had in common was that each of us had left our former lives and careers to serve as United States Peace Corps Volunteers.

I found it especially interesting to learn about the experiences of this eclectic group, and what had brought them to this particular juncture. One woman had spent eight years in Africa as a volunteer with Habitat for Humanity International, and now this chatty, interesting, intrepid woman in her late 40s was off on another incredible adventure.

To me, all of the people in Group 14 were exceptional, unique, and talented. They would each bring special gifts to their Peace Corps service, and a few would become good friends and invaluable resources in the months to come.

Peter Brown (my game partner) was a graduate of Hobart College in upstate New York. Despite his young years, he was immensely wise, perhaps even the smartest in the group. When Peter spoke, everyone listened. You knew that whatever he had to say would be worthwhile. He was also funny, personable, and kind.

Sean Anderson was a 30-something from San Diego. In his former life, he had been a hazardous materials inspector. He was an avid tennis player and looked forward to playing on the clay courts in Romania.

Beth Haskovec would end up in my language group. Although only in her early 20s, she had already amassed a wealth of world experience. After graduating from the University of Northern Iowa, she had volunteered for AmeriCorps, where she had been the director of a literacy program. Beth had a huge philanthropic heart, and said she could not remember a time in her life when she and her family were not volunteering in some capacity.

Diane Turkin was a 50-something redheaded firecracker with an infectious laugh and a tell-it-like-it-is attitude. An immunologist by profession, Diane was from the New York/New Jersey area and had two college-age sons.

At noon the next day, we boarded two chartered buses for Dulles International Airport. There were still 40 of us; there had been no defections during the night. Clearing security was a two-hour process. At the check-in counter, Austrian Airlines wanted to charge me again for my excess luggage. No thanks, I said under my breath. I already gave in Austin.

What I said out loud was, "Look at all these people! Some only have one bag, some have two. Can't we just average it out and call it even? Besides, I'm going to Romania as a Peace Corps Volunteer . . ."

They let me board without paying the surcharge. I was finally on my way to Romania.

3
Ploiesti: Arrival in an Alien Land

Ploiesti, February 16, 2002

> *Once we settled into our hotel, the Peace Corps wasted no time in launching our cultural education. Our first two days were filled with orientations, medical briefings, and, yes, shots. So far this week, I've received polio and hepatitis A and B immunizations. I am one of the lucky ones. Others received many more. The orientation sessions are daunting; there is no slacking or sleeping late. And Romanian toilet paper feels like sandpaper.*

I arrived in Bucharest with my backpack, 240 pounds of luggage, and a huge rush of adrenaline. It was February 15th of the second year of the new millennium.

As the plane banked for landing, I heard the familiar strains of the Beach Boys over the sound system. I wasn't sure if this was a "Welcome" for the Americans on board, or just an indication of the international appeal of this popular band, but I was pretty sure it would be a long time before I heard their music again.

The moment we touched down at Otopeni International Airport, all my old doubts came bubbling up. I was suddenly unsure whether my decision to join the Peace Corps was the smartest thing I had ever done or unbelievably stupid. I was about to find out.

The airport, recently renamed after Henry Coanda, the Romanian aerodynamics pioneer and inventor of the jet engine, was surprisingly modern and efficient. I remembered a Czech train ride from Munich to Prague just a year earlier and how "communist" everything had seemed. I had expected the same in Bucharest because of its communist history, but the government had been busy erasing the past.

After clearing customs, we boarded two modern, American-style tour buses for the hour-long ride to Ploiesti, where we would spend the next ten weeks in pre-service training. As I was leaving the terminal, I heard someone call my name. I was sure no one in Bucharest knew me, but apparently someone did. It was Tina Covaci, the environmental program manager for Peace Corps Romania. She had received a copy of an article that had appeared in my hometown newspaper, and she had recognized me from my photo. It wasn't a red-carpet sighting, but it felt like one.

The afternoon was cold and gray, the sky overcast, the bus thankfully warm. Along the way, we passed a few horse-drawn wagons that were seemingly oblivious to the traffic that swirled around them. I was undeniably in an alien place.

Ploiesti was a somber, sprawling city; an oil town colored in shades of gray, the cityscape a blend of crumbling communist-era apartments, shabby modern buildings, and belching oil refineries. Many of the city's beautiful old buildings had been lost to war and neglect. I would soon be living in one of those Soviet-style apartment buildings.

Most of the city's 300,000-plus inhabitants appeared to be cruising the congested, potholed streets in an assortment of aging vehicles. Bicycles, cars, trucks, and buses rattled along perilously close to each other in a confused maze. On the street corners, peasant women in heavy coats, thick stockings, and babushkas were selling tiny white flowers called *ghiocei* (snowdrop) for 3,000 lei, or about five cents. I can still smell the lovely fragrance of these sweet harbingers of spring.

The world's first oil production began in Ploiesti in 1857, and the city has been pumping oil out of the porous limestone rock beneath the flat Prahova plain ever since. By 1942, Ploiesti was Europe's second-largest oil producer (the Soviet Union was first), producing nearly a million tons of oil each month. In 1943, Ploiesti refineries were providing almost a third of the oil that powered the Nazi war machine. At that time, few

Americans except for Allied war planners had ever heard of Ploiesti.

During World War II, Romania was the target of one of the war's most daring long-range bombing raids. On August 1, 1943, 178 American Liberator B-24 bombers took off from North Africa, their target the German-controlled refineries in Ploiesti. The raid destroyed nearly half the production capacity. Ploiesti was the most heavily damaged Romanian city in World War II.

Although the attack was a major setback to Hitler's war effort, the cost was steep. Of the 178 planes and 1,726 men who had taken off on the mission, 52 planes and 530 men failed to return.

* * *

At the Hotel Prahova where we would spend our first two nights, we were given our room keys and some pocket money. The single phone-booth-size elevator was barely big enough for me and one suitcase, so I had to make three trips. My room was spare but adequate, with European-style twin beds, thin wool blankets, a nightstand, and worn carpeting. Two coat hooks behind the door provided the only closet.

Shortly after we checked into our rooms, a Ploiesti Peace Corps Volunteer announced, "If anyone wants a little tour of this town, meet me here after dinner." I wasn't going to pass this up. A little after 7:00 p.m., 15 of us ventured out into the raw February slush to savor some local culture. We ended up in a tiny, smoke-filled pub full of warm cheer and cold beer. I bought a draft of local brew for about 50 cents US. During my time in Ploiesti, I would drink a lot of beer in that pub.

After a few hours, I began to feel the effects of 36 hours without sleep. Fatigue, emotional overload, and a lingering sore throat had exhausted all my reserves. I headed back to the hotel and was asleep almost before my head hit the pancake-flat pillow.

Our first full day in Romania began promptly at 8:00 a.m. the next morning. Forty tired but enthusiastic recruits gathered in the hotel conference room after breakfast for the health and safety session. We were warmly welcomed by Dr. Dan, a charismatic Romanian with twinkling eyes, a disarming manner, and the title of Peace Corps medical officer (PCMO). Because Romanian medical facilities and practices in 2002 were generally not up to Western standards, the Peace Corps maintained its own medical contractor and health unit in Bucharest to provide health care for the Romanian Volunteers.

Dr. Dan set the tone right away. "Expensive bags like that red one do not have any place here in Romania. You are asking for that bag to be snatched."

It was my bag he was talking about.

"Always be aware that, as an American, you're a target," he continued.

We were told not to drink the tap water because of possible lead contamination, and were each issued a water filter and a first-aid kit. The good doctor also warned us about eating fish, since origins were questionable and could possibly be the nearby Danube River, which was extremely polluted. We learned that fresh fruits and vegetables were readily available during the summer months, but in short supply during the winter. There would be plenty to eat, but the variety would be limited, particularly in the smaller towns.

At noon, we sat down to a lunch of fresh cheese and salami, followed by a sour soup, chicken schnitzel, boiled potatoes, and cake. While the fare was not exactly Continental, the portions were generous and the food surprisingly good. I would later learn that the deliciously sour taste of Romanian soups comes from lemons or more commonly, from fermented wheat bran.

During orientation, all our meals were served in the hotel dining room. The buffet-style breakfast included cold meats, salty cheeses, bread, tomatoes, and yogurt. The menu did not vary. Lunch consisted of soup and a hot meat dish. Dinner was similar to lunch. Desserts were the most disappointing. They always looked tempting, but were drenched in water rather than the syrup I expected.

That night I dreamed about Mexican quesadillas and German chocolate cake.

4

Life with My Gazda

Ploiesti, February 20, 2002

I will be a Peace Corps "Trainee" for 10 weeks, and the best part of my training will be living with a Romanian host family, an arrangement that will help me acclimate to Romanian life and learn the language more quickly. I cannot imagine how difficult it must be to open your home to a complete stranger — and a foreign one at that — but my courageous host family (gazda in Romanian) has done just that. My gazda is a single mom with a 12-year-old son. Dana is a petroleum engineer for Rompetrol, the national petroleum company. Vlad is a quiet, shy sixth-grader who enjoys many of the same things that teenagers in the U.S. enjoy: computer games, TV, basketball, and hanging with friends. Although Dana will receive a stipend from the Peace Corps for my meals and accommodation, her decision to welcome me into her home was really all about expanding her world and embracing new experiences.

On Sunday morning, all the Peace Corps Trainees (we would not be called Volunteers until after our training) gathered in the hotel lobby and waited anxiously to meet the families with whom we would spend the next two-and-a-half months. Some people were quite astonished by the amount of luggage we had, or rather, by the amount of luggage *I* had.

Before leaving the States, I had filled out several questionnaires. The information I provided would help the Peace Corps place me in a compatible living situation (smoker, non-smoker, etc.). One question even asked about food preferences. I did not like beets, but I had failed to mention that I did not like liver either, so whenever I was served liver at my *gazda's* home, I had to eat it. And smile.

In evaluating prospective living accommodations for volunteers, the Peace Corps typically considers such factors as access to banking, medical, and postal services; availability of public transportation and communications; and proximity to other volunteers. In Romania, there was also a full-time Peace Corps staff member assigned to *gazda* relations.

The Peace Corps screens its host families thoroughly, visiting their homes and interviewing the families before placing a volunteer. Lodging requirements differ from country to country, depending on how the host-country nationals live. In return for a generous stipend, the family is required to provide their Peace Corps guest with three meals a day and a private room with a bed and a door that closes, a task that was not always easy. It was not uncommon for a host family to have as many as four people living in a one-bedroom apartment, in which case the entire family slept in the living room while the guest got the bedroom. When there were no guests, the children usually slept in the bedroom, while the parents slept on a foldout in the living room.

* * *

From the moment I saw Dana, I loved her. She had learned about the Peace Corps program from her neighbor, who had hosted several PCTs. Three years earlier while on vacation in Greece, Dana's husband dove into a swimming pool, broke his neck, and died — right in front of Dana and her son. Dana was 33; Vlad was nine. Dana had decided that hosting a PCT might be a good thing, especially for 12-year-old Vlad.

While I was in Ploiesti, Dana would be my friend, my inspiration, and my soulmate. Dressed in sensible shoes and Euro-chic clothes, she was tall, bubbly, and utterly endearing, with laughing eyes, dark hair, deep dimples, and a contagious laugh. The other volunteers immediately dubbed her "hot." Confident, smart, and ambitious, Dana worked two jobs, looked after her aging parents, and still managed to shop at the market and cook dinner for Vlad and me every night.

The apartment was small by American standards (maybe not by New York City standards), with two bedrooms, a living room, a bath and a half (unusual in Romania), a small kitchen, and the ubiquitous balcony. There was a small wooden table and stools in the kitchen, and obligatory white lace curtains on every window (common in Romania, even in schools and public buildings). In the living room, a landscape painting in an ornate gold frame hung on the bare concrete wall above a comfortable couch. A small TV occupied a shelf in a large wood cabinet, and Dana's bookshelves held hundreds of books. In fact, almost every Romanian had hundreds of books.

Television programs included Romanian HBO (no *Sex and the City*, but movies in English with Romanian subtitles), International CNN, the Cartoon Network, the Romanian version of *Who Wants to be a Millionaire*, and the Discovery Channel.

Vlad had kindly given me his room for my 10-week visit. He would sleep in his mother's bedroom, and at the end of my stay, would be rewarded with something new for his room.

The first evening, Dana prepared a delicious dinner of soup and schnitzel. Afterwards, she and Vlad took me on a walk through the chilly February dusk to show me how to find the school where I would begin my training classes the next morning.

An excellent cook, Dana refused to let me help her in the kitchen (or anywhere else, for that matter). We ate lots of meat, bread, and potatoes, but my favorite meal was *mamaliga,* a delicious Romanian staple of steamed corn meal covered with salty homemade cheese and sour cream. Romanian coffee is drunk Turkish-style, strong, black, and very sweet, and although I do not drink coffee, I was always offered a cup.

The next morning, I met Vlad's paternal grandmother, a short, sturdy woman with mischievous blue eyes and an impish smile. Usually attired in heavy winter stockings, oversized sweater, and furry Cossack hat, Buni was incredibly kind to me. Every morning she came to stay with Vlad until he went to school after lunch. She would fix my breakfast and pack a lunch for me to take to school. Wrapped up snugly in a paper towel, my lunch of bread, butter, salami, and cheese seldom varied. Each morning Buni gave me the weather report, checking my outfit to be sure

I was appropriately dressed. Buni didn't speak English, but we managed to make ourselves understood with lots of gestures and giggles.

Dana (and all the host families) had been instructed by the Peace Corps to boil our drinking water and then filter it through the PC-supplied water filter. The host families simply accepted that we could not drink their water. The Peace Corps had explained that since we had not grown up in Romania, there might be organisms in the water that our bodies were not accustomed to. Buni had a full pot of filtered water ready for me every morning.

Dana spoke very little English, and I spoke no Romanian, but from the beginning, communication was not a problem. Every evening after dinner, we sat around the tiny kitchen table with the Romanian/English dictionary and spent hours talking, gesturing, and laughing in our Romanenglish as we struggled to learn from each other.

The apartment began to feel oddly like home, my other life slowly slipping away.

5
Boot Camp

Ploiesti, February 25, 2002
> *The training we had all been anxiously anticipating began in earnest on Monday morning. Classes are held all day Monday through Friday and on most Saturday mornings. From 8:00 a.m. till noon, we attend language classes at the local elementary school. We eat lunch in our classroom, then travel to the high school for our technical classes. We meet together as a group one afternoon a week and all day on Friday. We have a LOT of assignments and homework, and I am working harder here than I ever did in college. With all the training and support at hand, it is hard to imagine that I might fail, but I am well aware of the possibility.*

A combination of college, boot camp, and Outward Bound, Peace Corps training is unlike any other. Designed to inspire, educate, and equip you to adapt and survive in your new culture, the training is also an opportunity for the Peace Corps to identify your strengths as well as your weaknesses.

The first few weeks of training felt sort of like swimming with floaties. The staff guided and supported us as we found our way, making sure that we did not flounder. Our courses included Romanian language, cross-cultural studies, and technical training in our appropriate fields (mine was environmental), as well as safety and security issues. Proficiency in the Romanian language would be essential to the success of my service, and I would have to meet specific language requirements if I ever wished to change my status from Trainee to Volunteer.

The cross-cultural classes compared Romanian and American values, attitudes, and customs. Living with my Romanian family would be a central part of this training, providing total immersion in culture as well as language.

All classes except for language studies were held at a local high school (the Peace Corps called it the Hub) on the third floor of the girls' dormitory. Boarding facilities were common where high schools were far apart. I found the "Ally McBeal" bathrooms a bit challenging at first. I had always viewed the idea of a shared bathroom (with stalls for both men and women) as an interesting concept on TV, but to experience it firsthand gave me a new appreciation for personal space. Nevertheless, I approached the situation with equanimity and simply remembered my Outward Bound experience. If I could spend eight days at sea with no facilities, I could do the unisex thing.

The technical practicum included staff observations and feedback, all designed to help us build the confidence and skills we would need to be successful. In all our efforts, we were supported by very capable Romanian instructors, Peace Corps staff, and in-service volunteers. It was hard to imagine that we would soon be swimming without our floaties.

As part of our safety training, we were required to attend a session about safe sex. Dr. Dan lectured and offered statistics on how many of us would be having sex by the time we closed our service. Then we played a game in which he asked a question and tossed condoms to those who got the answer correct. He also tossed condoms to those who did *not* answer, due either to lack of knowledge, sheer embarrassment, or the belief that you would not be sexually active as a volunteer.

Fortunately, our class did not have to actually practice any safe sex techniques. We heard that in another group, everyone had to practice putting a condom on a banana to ensure that, should the need arise (pun intended), they could, um, put a condom on a banana.

* * *

34

I have always been a klutz. I fall down a lot — sprawling to the ground, never pretty. I had been in Romania for almost two weeks before it happened, and the event was long overdue. While I was walking from the Hub to the bus stop with another trainee, I stepped off the curb and fell right into a puddle of brown slush. My pants and coat were soaked but it was my ego that suffered the most. At home, I got a lot of sympathy from Dana. The next morning, while Buni was making my breakfast, she told me that she had heard about my fall, and was thrilled with its portent. Apparently, my fall was a sign. What kind of sign? A sign that I would get married soon — to a Romanian.

Right, Buni, I thought. Not likely.

Cash only, and lots of it

In 2002, Romania was basically a cash society — no bank accounts, no personal checks, and only limited credit card use. To me, everything seemed to cost thousands. In fact, everything really *did* cost thousands of lei. In 2002, a single US dollar was worth about 33,000 lei.[1] Everyone simply carried around great bundles of bills. Although many places displayed Visa and MasterCard signs, these seemed to serve merely as decoration. There were money exchanges everywhere, and Romanians seemed to prefer other currencies to their own, probably due to the constantly fluctuating lei and lack of trust in the banking system. Most Romanians simply converted their lei into other currencies and kept their stash at home. You could, however, use your debit or credit card to withdraw cash (in lei) from the numerous ATM machines. Interestingly, all cell phone plans were priced in US dollars.

While we were in training, the Peace Corps paid our expenses and gave us the equivalent of $25 a week in pocket money. That didn't seem like much, but with chips costing about 30 cents (10,000 lei) and beer only about 50 cents, I managed quite well. We ate out rarely, bought hot, fresh donuts occasionally, and went out for beer a lot. During the first few weeks, I was able to save enough money to buy a cell phone.

Overall, Romania was an inexpensive country. In the larger cities, however, prices were more in line with Western economies. Major hotels and services charged major prices, but there were reasonably priced Euro-style hotels all over the country. For about $12 to $20 US, you could find a clean, basic room with a bath down the hall. You could take a taxi across Ploiesti for about $1 US. Amazingly, despite the fact that I was obviously American (and therefore loaded), no one ever tried to take advantage of me in Romania.

Transportation

Public transportation was quite adequate via bus, trolley, or tram. You could get just about anywhere you needed to go, but not necessarily quickly. Dana had a car, but most Romanians did not. I should point out that in Romania, you do not drink and drive. If you had a drink — just a single one — you didn't drive. Period. The penalties were severe and no one was willing to risk the outcome. As a Peace Corps Volunteer, I was not allowed to own or drive a car or motorcycle, or to ride as a passenger on a motorcycle.

Shoe shock

The shoes worn by Romanian women did not escape my admiration or my curiosity. I watched in utter amazement as women walked up and down steep steps and over cobbled, potholed streets and sidewalks in the highest heels, the tallest boots, the pointiest toes, and the fanciest pumps I had ever seen. These shoes should have come with a hazard warning and supplemental oxygen, but I never saw anyone wearing this remarkable footwear take a tumble.

Noise, smoke, confusion

New movies arrived in Romanian theaters anywhere from three to six months after they were released in the United States. I had been to two movies in Ploiesti since my arrival and both times, it was an enlightening experience. Forget about stadium seating, smokeless venues, common courtesy, and silence during a movie. Instead, think noise, confusion, smoke, and continuous cell phone conversations.

The movie theaters I visited were huge and reminded me of the cavernous old movie houses of days gone by. There were probably over a thousand seats as well as a balcony (which was where most people wanted to sit). Smoking was allowed (seemingly required), cell phones were never turned off, and everyone talked during the feature presentation. And if you happened to be in a group of three or more people, you would never find seats together since so many of them were broken. If the movie had already started and you needed to find your mates, no problem. Just yell out their names in your best football-stadium voice. To blend in here, you needed to have your cell phone ringtone set at the highest volume so that when it rang during the movie, everyone in the theater knew you were getting a call. You also had to speak very loudly into your phone to your boyfriend, mistress, or wife so that everyone could hear your business. I personally believe that since the movies were mainly in English (with Romanian subtitles), moviegoers did not need to listen; they only had to watch the action, read the subtitles, and talk away.

Flashing the Romanians

I'm sure I must have looked rather odd as I walked to school every day with my backpack (unheard of for adults in Romania), while practicing Romanian with my homemade flash cards. I used my flash cards often because Romanian is a difficult language to learn (at least for me). There are 28 letters in the Romanian alphabet and there is no y or q. There are more vowels than we English speakers are used to, and they sound different from English vowels. Even the word order is different. I was glad my language class had only five students.

As I made my way around Ploiesti, I eavesdropped on conversations wherever I could, on the bus, in a restaurant, at the market, trying to make out words I could recognize. One word that sounded surprisingly familiar was *fac*. This word is pronounced exactly like the American slang word that begins with the same letter. In Romanian, *fac* means "to make." Every time I used it, I cringed, and *fac* was a word that was used often. Eventually, the word rolled off my tongue like I was a seasoned sailor.

On my way to school one day, an older woman came up beside me and spoke to me in Romanian. It was obvious I was not Romanian but she wanted to know who I was and why I was in Romania. She spoke little English and I spoke even less Romanian. She eventually came to understand that I was a Peace Corps Volunteer from the United States. I eventually understood that she wanted me to come to her house and meet her son. As we walked along, she hooked her arm through mine. This appealing custom was common among Romanian women.

[1] *On July 1, 2005, four zeros were dropped from the lei (i.e., one U.S. dollar would equal 29,200 old lei or 2.92 new lei). On December 31, 2006, the old currency was withdrawn.*

6
Superstitions, Gypsies, and Orphans

Ploiesti, March 2002
　Nu ma pot plange. *I cannot complain. I have now been here about two weeks and, much to my surprise, I am adapting well. In spite of new challenges, a new language, and new surroundings, I sleep well, pay attention in school, and study hard each evening. My mother would be proud. What I really miss are my friends. And peanut butter and American toilet paper.*

Every day brought new experiences as well as subtle reminders of what I had left behind. Before I got to Romania, I thought a lot about how I was going to wash my clothes. Most Romanians did not have automatic washers, and automatic dryers were non-existent. I was lucky, at least for the training period, to have an automatic washer at Dana's apartment. It worked much like its American counterpart, but was much smaller. My challenge was drying my clothes. Everything was hung up to dry outside on the balcony. We lived on a busy street and I wasn't at all sure I wanted to hang my panties out for all of Ploiesti to see. So I made a point of hanging my shirts and pants on the line closest to the street, putting the more intimate items on the inside row. Of course, this allowed everyone in the living room a perfect view, but the audience was considerably smaller.

There were several Romanian customs I found interesting, if not totally bizarre. For example, Romanians believe that sitting in a cross draft or "current" — in a house, building, train, bus, taxi, anywhere — is a bad thing and can cause numerous infirmities like sore throats, backaches, and earaches. Doors were always shut, and most rooms had doors. Any attempt to open a window on a sweltering train or bus was met with anxious gestures and angry reprimands.

But the "spitting" custom (and I don't mean spitting on the street, which men did regularly) was baffling. If you cooed over a baby, a lamb, a calf, or any young creature, you also had to spit. But no spittle should actually leave your mouth. This has to do with the belief that too much adoration will make the young creature sick and spitting somehow counters the harm done by this admiration. Dana and I spent at least an hour one evening with the Romanian/English dictionary laughing and spitting, while trying to sort it all out.

And don't ever sit at the corner of a table, as this will surely end any opportunities for marriage.

Martisor

The traditional celebration honoring spring is called *Martisor* (from the Romanian word for March, *Martie*), celebrated on March 1. On this day, it is customary for women and girls to be given little charms called *martisors*, typically a small flower or trinket, often tied with red and white thread. As the legend goes, those who wear these little talismen will be happy, healthy, and strong in the year to come. The town square in Ploiesti was filled with little kiosks selling these lovely little charms. I was pinned all over, delighted to receive *martisors* from my classmates as well as from Dana, Buni, and Vlad.

Dog days

Large numbers of scrappy stray dogs roamed Ploiesti, as they did in most major cities in Romania. I encountered the dogs daily and listened to them nightly. During Ceausescu's regime, many private houses had been destroyed and the owners forced into apartment blocs, leaving their beloved pets behind. The progeny of these abandoned animals were largely harmless scavengers, but they were a major nuisance. To cope with the problem, we used Peace Corps-issued dog repellent, which emitted a high-frequency sound to distract the dogs. I carried mine with me at all times but never had to use it._

Several years before, in an effort to reduce the escalating dog population, the mayor of Bucharest ordered thousands of dogs rounded up and euthanized, an action that incurred the wrath of many citizens. Romania's love/hate attitude toward the homeless dogs is not surprising, considering their history and inherent empathy with the discarded and neglected.

A trip to Billa

One Sunday, Sean (another PCT) and I decided to make a trip to Billa. Billa was a big deal. It was the only "supermarket" in Ploiesti, about half the size of a typical American supermarket, but in Romania, this was huge. Our intention was not to buy, but to browse. But when I spotted the lemon Fanta and hazelnut yogurt, I bought. Billa stocked a few American items like Philadelphia Cream Cheese and M&Ms, but they were pricey. There was a variety of pork sausages and chops, and milk was not refrigerated (until opened). Green veggies were limited and expensive at Billa, but the open markets had a nice selection of reasonably priced carrots, radishes, cucumbers, and lettuce.

Romania's gypsies

Romania is home to more than 2 million gypsies, the largest single population of Roma in the world. Exotic, colorful, and darker-skinned than most Romanians, Roma are typically very poor and often the target of irrational hostility. Ironically, gypsy musicians are highly valued as performers. I would often see Roma children begging in the streets, many of them taught from the cradle to beg.

Once when I was talking on a pay phone to a friend in the States, a young Roma child and her barefoot, infant-toting mother approached me and began kissing my feet and crossing themselves. The child knew how to say, "I'm hungry" in English, and he could cry crocodile tears. When it became apparent that I wasn't going to give them any money, their disappointment was obvious and mean-spirited.

Ever since the first Gypsy walked out of India over a thousand years ago, they have survived without homeland or government to safeguard their interests. Determined to preserve their own unique customs, their survival is due in large part to a strong sense of brotherhood and a fiercely guarded culture cloaked in secrecy. After decades of being denied education, employment, and even marginal membership in society, many Roma defiantly embrace theft and begging as entitlement.

Despite the stereotypes, there are many successful Roma. One of the Peace Corps' Romanian language teachers was Roma and taught English at a local high school. Then there is Madalin Voicu, a world-renowned musician and one of the best-known Roma politicians in Romania. Voicu has served as conductor of the Symphonic Orchestra in Ploiesti, as a member of the Romanian parliament (1996–2004), and as director of the award-winning Bucharest Chamber Orchestra, founded by his father in 1969.

On-site training

About five weeks into training, the Peace Corps sends you on a site visit to observe how other volunteers actually live and work. So in mid-March, my language class (all five of us) and our instructor traveled to Resita, near the Serbian/Montenegro border, for a glimpse of the Peace Corps at work.

We left Saturday night, planning to return the following Wednesday. The journey by overnight train took over eight hours. I actually slept well on the train, probably due to the monotony of the clackity-clack, or maybe it was the wine I drank.

Sitting in a geographical bowl surrounded by the foothills of the Transylvanian Alps, Resita was very polluted and visibly poor. In a former life, Resita had been a prosperous steel town (steam locomotives were manufactured there from 1872 to 1964), but most of the plants were now closed. An American company had purchased one such plant, but even it had recently shut down. The citizens had protested against this perceived American injustice only days before our visit.

In Resita, we visited five in-service volunteers. Seeing the organizations they served and the apartments in which they lived, I understood exactly what Dorothy in *The Wizard of Oz* meant when she said "this isn't Kansas anymore." Their offices were cold, dingy converted apartments with little in the way of furniture or office equipment. Yet what these organizations and their small staffs lacked in material items, they more than made up for in passion for their work.

After visiting the volunteers' apartments, I was encouraged by thoughts of what mine might look like. Housed in the ubiquitous concrete bloc buildings, the apartments were comfortable and spacious, typically furnished with a foldout couch in the living area and a small table and stools in the kitchen. The doors to the rooms opened onto a foyer containing a full-wall coat rack and a place for shoes. And each volunteer's apartment was filled with something that no typical Romanian apartment would have — the cherished mementos of the American tenants, each item representing what and who was special and significant back home.

One of the organizations we visited was a caving group committed to preserving Romania's beautiful natural caverns. Another organization helped older orphans make the transition into society. In Romania, once an orphan turns 18, he or she is literally turned out into the street with no skills, no job prospects, and no support — utterly alone. Many of the boys become factory workers or join the military where, because they have no family to care about them, they are given the most dangerous jobs. Most of the girls face an equally grim future as prostitutes.

Three Romanian employees of this seriously under-funded organization worked without pay because they were so dedicated to the orphans. These were not rich people, and they struggled to put food on their own tables. But there was some good news for this group: They had recently received a grant to establish a farm so the orphans could learn skills in agriculture and related businesses. Small stipends for the staff were also included.

During one of our training meetings, I was introduced to a young Romanian doctor who cared for patients from the local schools and factories. I asked her what kinds of illnesses she typically treated. Most recently, she had treated two children suffering from malnutrition, who had not eaten in several days.

We had language classes every morning we were in Resita, as well as on the train going back to Ploiesti. I found this rather amusing since, as Americans, we already attracted enough attention. The mobile language lessons merely sharpened the focus.

The train ride offered a brief respite from the realities of Peace Corps service. The countryside we saw from the train windows was a postcard-perfect landscape of gently rolling hills and picturesque villages. It was springtime in the valley, the orchards and trees were full of blossoms, and the peasants were just beginning to work the fields.

The peasant culture is still an important part of Romanian society, and many of the farmers live today just as they have for centuries, relying on horse-drawn plows, wooden tools, and manual labor to plant and harvest their crops. There appeared to be no age or gender boundaries. Men and women, young and old (some in their 60s and 70s), worked long hours on the land and the fruits of their labor often ended up in the local markets. It seemed to me that Romanians labored exceptionally hard in the 21st Century, while there were so many conveniences available in other parts of the world.

7
The Funeral

Dana's mother died of cancer about six weeks into my Romanian service. She had been diagnosed in January, just before my February arrival. But even with this devastating news, Dana still welcomed an unknown American into her home and into her life. In Romania, cancer is a death sentence since people usually wait too long to see a doctor about their symptoms. They know that if it is anything serious, they might not have money for the bribes required to receive good care.

Dana became her mother's caregiver. Every day on her way home from work, she would stop by her parents' house, fix dinner, and attend to her mother's needs. Then she would come home and fix dinner for Vlad and me. Never complaining, she did what was needed and still made me feel like a welcome member of the family.

When I arrived back in Ploiesti after my trip to Resita, Dana was not home, but Buni was. This was unusual since Buni usually came in the morning and left when Vlad went to school. Buni explained that Dana's mother had passed away and the funeral was the next day. My Romanian language skills were still pretty limited and I was not at all sure that I understood. She then showed me a flyer with the funeral information. Seeing the words on paper helped me to fully understand what had happened, and what was going to happen.

My instinct in situations like this is to do something, to bake, to order flowers, to do all the things that Americans do when someone dies. But in Romania, I had no idea what was culturally correct.

Buni wanted me to eat. Even during this difficult time, she had made delicious cabbage rolls for me, but I was not hungry. I thought about my own mother thousands of miles away, and how I would feel if this were my loss. Old feelings of personal sorrow bubbled up as I remembered my father's death when I was a child. I ate Buni's special food, which she had prepared with such unselfishness. I understood that "doing" during difficult times can be cathartic.

After dinner, I called the Peace Corps office to get more information (in English) about what was culturally appropriate in this situation. The duty officer walked me through the death and funeral customs. I decided that I would not go to training the next day so I could attend the funeral. Arrangements were made for me to ride to the funeral with Leo, one of Dana's friends.

When Dana came home late that night, I was already asleep. I was sure she had spent most of the night comforting her father and making funeral preparations. Romanians prepare the body of the deceased at home. The coffin is delivered to your residence, and the family cleans, dresses, and arranges the body for burial.

Sometime during the night, I became ill, shuffling to and from the bathroom numerous times. When I got up in the morning, Dana was already awake. I told her how sorry I was for her loss and embraced her. Despite her ordeal, she looked stunning. But even in her grief, she was still concerned about me. She had heard my trips to the bathroom in the night and was worried about my health. I assured her I was fine and would see her at the funeral.

Now I needed to convince myself that I was fine. I got out my Peace Corps-issued first-aid kit and took some stomach medicine. Eating was the last thing on my mind, so I settled for some water and a piece of bread.

I put on the only nice outfit I had brought from home, a green-and-black herringbone suit with a faux fur collar. Leo picked me up along with three of Dana's co-workers and we headed for the flower market. The Peace Corps office had explained the tradition of funeral flowers: You give an even number of flowers for memorial services; odd numbers are for the living. Leo helped me select the right number of flowers. Dana's colleagues pooled their money and bought a wreath with a ribbon that said simply "Rest in Peace."

The funeral was held in the chapel at the cemetery. I looked around anxiously to see if there were "facilities" in the area but I saw none. I prayed that I would not need any. The chapel was small, about the size of a large bedroom in the U.S., and there were no pews. In Romanian churches, this is the custom. The simple pine coffin lay in the middle of the room, the lid off to the side. The mourners gathered around the coffin, quickly filling the small room.

Leo guided me through the ritual of placing half my flowers on one side of the body, the rest on the other side. Dana's mother looked peaceful in a simple black dress, her hands clutching a lighted candle, white lace surrounding her.

As I looked around at the other mourners, I realized immediately that I did not "blend" in. And it wasn't just because I was the only American. Although I had worn the only nice outfit I had, I was definitely out of place in my very American dress-up outfit. Even Dana wore simple black slacks and a black shirt.

The service finally began, the flickering candles quickly heating the still air in the tiny room. I suddenly felt dizzy and lightheaded, and the thought that I might faint horrified me. I already attracted attention, just by being a redheaded American in my gauche clothes. I could imagine the attention I would get when I passed out at the funeral, but I made it through the service without incident.

The service was very emotional, with women wailing and men crying openly. At first this outpouring of sadness startled me, but it soon became a touching requiem for the deceased soul. At the end of the service, in keeping with Romanian tradition, the family gave small tokens to the mourners. I received some fruit and a white linen handkerchief with a coin tucked inside (sort of like a toll to cross over to the other side). Sweet grains and wine were also offered.

After the service, they took the coffin outside to the burial site. The grave had been dug by hand early in the morning and the dirt was piled along side. The lid was placed on the coffin and one of the cemetery workers began to nail the coffin shut. With each strike of the hammer, the death seemed more final. The coffin was lowered into the ground with ropes and the priest gave his final blessing. The service was over.

Later that evening, Dana come into my room and sat on the bed. She had brought me some tea to settle my stomach. She had just buried her mother, yet she was comforting me. As I sipped the tea, Dana asked me, "What are funerals like in America?"

I told her that grief was universal and that we each handled it in our own way. I explained that, in the U.S., we sat in pews in our churches and synagogues and dabbed our eyes and tried to hold back our tears. I told her how moved I had been by the beauty of her mother's service and the outpouring of emotion. We talked and cried together for almost an hour, and I hold that memory in my heart as if it happened yesterday.

8
Giurgiu

Ploiesti, April 2002

This is our last week of training. Yesterday, we were all tested orally on our language skills and rated accordingly. The Peace Corps would like you to leave training with a "novice-high" rating. I am proud to say I surpassed that goal. I still have a long way to go before I can function at the 50-percent rate, but I now have a good base on which to build my fluency when I get to my permanent site.

At the end of April, spring finally arrived. Overnight, Ploiesti went from wintry gray to a city in bloom. The main boulevard was lined with budding trees and colorful flowers, and the fountains were about to spring forth. I would be sad to leave Ploiesti; I had made many good friends during my ten-week stay, and I would miss this time and this place.

Ever since I had arrived in Romania, I had wondered *where* I would be assigned for my two years of service. Peace Corps trainees are not assigned to individual sites until well into their pre-service training. This gives the staff an opportunity to assess each trainee's technical and language skills in order to ensure the best match.

On Friday afternoon, the Peace Corps made the site announcements and I finally got my answer. I would spend the next two years in Giurgiu, a small city about an hour south of Bucharest. Located on the Bulgarian border along the famed Danube River (the only major European river to flow from west to east), Giurgiu had a population of about 70,000 and a history that dated back to the 1300s. The city had been conquered many times over by Turks, Russians, and Austrians, to name a few. Giurgiu had been badly damaged in 1916 during World War I, and had been heavily bombed by the Allies during World War II.

Considered the gateway between Europe and the Middle East, Giurgiu was a thriving port city. International trains originating in Belgium and terminating in Istanbul frequently traveled right through town. For hundreds of years, Giurgiu's most significant industry had been its shipyard. The first commercial sailing ship to fly the national flag was launched in Giurgiu, as well as the first steam-powered battle ship in 1862.

Giurgiu was also the first town in Romania to be honored by the U.S. Embassy with its "Doing Business Simply and Rapidly" award in 2001.

* * *

Initially, I was hugely disappointed in my assignment. The only place in Romania I did not want to be was near a river or along the coast. I would rather have lived without heat all winter than endure the summer heat and humidity guaranteed by proximity to water. On the pro side, Giurgiu was very close to Bucharest and I could cultivate relationships with the international media there. Being close to Bucharest would also make it easier for me to travel (to go anywhere, you must first go to Bucharest). So I decided to adopt the glass-half-full approach, look at the bright side, and withhold judgment, at least for the time being. I would also have to go on faith that I was being assigned there for a reason, and that the Peace Corps program manager felt my talents would be beneficial to this particular assignment. Besides, what didn't kill me would make me stronger, right? Wasn't Peace Corps service "the hardest job you will ever love?"

Over the weekend, all 40 of us visited our permanent sites. I traveled to Giurgiu with Lourrae, who would be my site mate, and we spent several days meeting with our counterparts, exploring the town, and preparing our apartments for the big move in two weeks. I was looking forward to getting back in a kitchen and cooking again.

I was lucky to have a Peace Corps sitemate; many volunteers did not. Always (yes, always) smiling and cheery, Lourrae would be a great friend and comfort during our service together. We got along well and it was nice to debrief and relieve stress in an English-only environment.

The Tourist Club, the organization to which I had been assigned, hosted a small dinner for us on Saturday night at one of the member's homes. The eclectic group numbered around 15, a handful of young people in junior high and high school, and a number of adults who had apparently been friends a long time.

I spent the evening observing the group. It seemed odd to see young people and adults socializing on the same level. Back home, the adults typically dominated a social gathering and the youth followed. Here, the school kids were an equal part of the group dynamic.

Ion, the club's leader, was a featured attraction — dynamic, charismatic, and very chummy with the girls. He was tall and slender and quite attractive until he opened his mouth and revealed that he was missing most of his teeth. Ion seemed to enjoy the attention, and he definitely had the pop-idol look going with his long ponytail and black leather pants. Months later, when I finally heard him sing in a band, my opinion quickly changed. Poor Ion was just a rock star wannabe who sang badly off-key.

Most of the group did not speak much English, but everyone seemed to knew just enough English or Romanian to understand each other. We ate pork chops and ice cream and warily took each other's measure. My observations from this evening would later reinforce my concerns about the club and its leadership.

Dr. Dan and his staff had already visited each of our apartments to ensure that they were suitable. I learned that I would be living in another apartment bloc and that — *omygosh!* — most of the people in Giurgiu did not have any hot water, unless they had an electric boiler, which most Romanians could not afford. But I would not be taking cold showers for long. The Peace Corps had given us the option of sharing the cost of a water heater with our Romanian organizations. I took them up on the offer and got my hot water. But only in the bathroom.

* * *

We had our final Hub session on Friday, and Peace Corps had saved the best for last. A local journalist was invited to present an overview of Romanian media before and after the revolution of 1989. If there was reason to criticize the Romanian media in 2002, it was nothing compared to how things had functioned before 1989. Diana showed us newspapers that had been published under the communist regime, full of glowing articles about the Ceausescus and the munificence of communism. "Life was colored pink and it was all a pink party."

In 2002, the government still largely controlled newspapers in Romania, but it was a vast improvement over the past. In November, Romania was to be considered, along with nine other countries, for membership in NATO. During the week of our last Hub session, NATO leaders were cautioning the Romanian government that more progress was needed toward judicial reform and the eradication of corruption before admission could be granted. Some even felt that there were still too many of the old regime in power. All of this was dutifully reported in the news, something that would never have happened just 13 years earlier.

The most compelling part of Diana's presentation was video footage from the Revolution. It was both fascinating and chilling, and I gained new insight into those five days in December that changed Romania forever.

* * *

I would miss riding the buses in Ploiesti. Always an adventure, the buses were only considered full when you could no longer shut the door and every inch of space on the inside was occupied. At times, the bus was so crowded I couldn't even get off at my stop. Eventually I learned to cement my feet to a spot near the door, forcing the new passengers to navigate around me. There were no "new" buses in Ploiesti, just castoffs from France, Germany, and other countries that had the resources to purchase new ones. Romania did not mind the second-hand vehicles; many of the country's buses and tramlines would not be operating at all if not for these multinational arrangements. And no one seemed terribly concerned that the maps, posters, and advertising signs from the original countries had been left — intact and in full color — on the buses. There were no Ploiesti maps on the buses in Ploiesti, but you could admire the ones from Germany and France all day long.

Prices in Romania

At first, things seemed relatively inexpensive to me. In reality, however, spending $10 dollars, or 320,000 lei, represented a huge chunk of my monthly income. (When I was in Romania, the U.S. dollar was equal to about 33,000 lei.) While in training, I received a stipend of approximately 800,000 lei a week, or about $25. This increased slightly when I arrived at my permanent site and had to pay my own living expenses. (PC volunteers were expected to live unassumingly as ordinary Romanian citizens.) Nevertheless, it took awhile to get used to shelling out thousands of lei for just a couple of items at the market.

Some examples of prices in Romania in 2002:

Item	Cost in U.S. $
One hour at Internet Café	.30
Movie admission	1.00
Taxi from Ploiesti to Bucharest airport	5.00
Small bag of potato chips	.20
Bus ticket in Ploiesti	.18
Maxi-taxi, Giurgiu to Bucharest	1.25
Big Mac Value Meal (McDonald's)	2.10
Bottle of soda (Fanta, Coke, etc.)	.35
Stamp to U.S.	1.63
Loaf of bread	.15
Double hotel room w/bath (Bucharest)	45.00
Double hotel room, no bath (Bucharest)	21.00
Bottled beer	1.00
Draft beer	.50

Something in the Pep — or the Bis

One morning, I woke up and my tongue was black. Not shades of black, not a little black, but black like night, like asphalt on the road, like my favorite summer sandals. I was more than a little freaked out when I went to brush my teeth and discovered what looked to me like a possible pre-plague condition. I felt fine and I looked fine, unless you looked inside my mouth. I immediately called my friend Julia (the chiropractic neurologist) and left a cryptic message on her machine back home in Texas. Julia called me back within a few minutes, but could offer no explanation. Her first response was not, "Oh my gosh, how horrible!" or "That is so awful!" Instead, she asked me, "Who else's tongue is black this morning, Lisa?" Julia was as perplexed as I was. I was sure I would lose my tongue by lunchtime. I thought about calling the medical office, but I would be going there for more immunizations later that day.

If this should ever happen to you, I know the explanation: Pepto-Bismol. That's right, the pink stuff. During the night, I had felt a bit nauseous so I chewed two of the pink tablets, and went back to sleep. You see, the active ingredient in Pepto-Bismol is bismuth. When a little bit of bismuth combines with the sulfur you might have in your saliva, a harmless but very black substance (bismuth sulfide) is produced. So said the Peace Corps medical authority.

Romanian rally drivers

Traveling by car in Romania can by terrifying. Put the most gentle, mild-mannered Romanian behind the wheel of a car and he or she turns into a hair-on-fire NASCAR driver, passing vehicles on blind curves at twice the legal speed. White lines may (or may not) be painted on the roads, but they indicate only the ability of the Romanians to paint white lines. Speed is determined by how far you can push the pedal down, and any pedestrian crossing the street risks certain death.

As in many places, there is a seat belt law, but like many laws in Romania, there is little enforcement and therefore little abiding. Parking was just as insane. If there was a flat surface, if your car could jump a curb or fit on a sidewalk, then that must be a parking space. The open space in the middle of the street was also considered a parking lot and it was sometimes hard to tell if a car or truck was parked or simply going very slow.

Romanian traffic laws are actually quite strict. Police can suspend your driver's license for up to three months for a number of indiscretions, including failure to yield, failure to stop at a red light, and failure to yield to pedestrians at a crosswalk. Driving under the influence of alcohol or causing an accident resulting in injury or death can mean serious consequences, even imprisonment. Despite the severe regulations, Romanian drivers exhibit an exceptionally cavalier attitude toward traffic laws.

9

The Mission Begins

Giurgiu, May 2002
> *It is hard for me to believe that training is finally over. The weeks have flown by but at times, they seemed like a lifetime. I have made valuable friendships, not only with Dana and Vlad, but with the other volunteers as well. The time I spent after school in the local pubs with the other trainees (cross-cultural training, right?) made me feel like a college student again. I've drunk more beer in the last 10 weeks than I have in the last 10 years. But now I am ready to begin what I came here to do. The Peace Corps encourages us to be innovative and independent in our assignments, sort of like writing and living by your own job description. The key to my success in the next two years will be my ability to adapt and to serve in this foreign land.*

On Friday, April 26, I took my Peace Corps oath along with 39 other proud classmates. The U.S. Ambassador, Michael Guest, and our *gazda* families were all there, along with the mayor and the local media. Afterwards, we had cookies and punch and congratulated each other.

I was part of the team that had been asked to speak at the ceremony. One volunteer thanked the Peace Corps staff, and two presented their entire speeches in Romanian, thanking the language instructors. When it was my turn, I thanked our *gazdas* (in English) and I only teared up once. The mayor of Ploiesti presented me with a massive bouquet of flowers because he "liked my speech."

Go figure.

Multumesc! **Thank You!**
Peace Corps Swearing-In Ceremony
Address presented by Lisa Fisher
Ploiesti, Romania. April 26, 2002

When I made the decision to join the Peace Corps, my friends and family told me how courageous I was. But any courage displayed by me or any of my colleagues was nothing compared to the courage that was displayed by our gazdas *in opening their homes and their hearts to complete strangers.*

Ten weeks ago, all of us stood in the lobby of the Hotel Prahova and waited anxiously to meet the families with whom we would spend the next 10 weeks. And when we each arrived at our respective homes, we found that not only were we welcomed with incredible hospitality, caring, and excitement, but also trusted immediately with the keys to their homes.

In many cases, families sacrificed their own comforts for ours. Many of the children happily gave up their rooms to the Americans who had come to stay with them. In our new environments, we quickly adapted to Romanian conventions like leaving our shoes at the door and avoiding "breezes" by not opening windows or doors, and were immediately immersed in the world's greatest hospitality, delicious food like mamaliga *and* sarmale, *and, of course,* tuica.

My favorite time at my gazda's home was dinner. This was family time, full of laughter, sharing, caring, and learning about each other's culture. I especially enjoyed sitting at the table after dinner with Dana and discussing what brought each one of us to this place in our lives. I arrived in Ploiesti a stranger, but I will leave knowing I am part of a family that has had a profound impact on my life, and who will always remain a part of my life.

To all our gazdas, we thank you. You have introduced us to the essence of what makes Romania such a wonderful place, the people. We thank you for all the food you prepared for us, for all the lunches you made, for caring about what we were wearing, for welcoming our friends, worrying about us, and making us special things when we were sick. But most important, we thank you for having the courage to open your home to a stranger. You are awesome. We love you. Multumesc!

Saying goodbye to the staff and the other volunteers was difficult, but finding the words to thank Dana, Vlad, and Buni was impossible. They had become a huge part of my life, and I could not imagine living without their daily comfort, humor, and support.

I knew that I would somehow have to transport all my possessions to my new apartment in Giurgiu (and my suitcases had grown much heavier over the past weeks). Most PCVs travel to their permanent sites via train or bus. The thought of making that trip with all my belongings seemed like a nightmare. But a friend of Dana's kindly drove me — and my suitcases — to Giurgiu in a sturdy Dacia station wagon. Dana and Vlad rode along.

* * *

My home in Giurgiu would be a drafty two-room apartment, where I would freeze during the long winter months and swelter during the stifling summers. And where I would experience the total absence of many of life's basic necessities like a clothes dryer, a microwave, reliable hot water, and soft toilet paper.

The apartment building appeared tired and shabby, but my second-floor flat was surprisingly large, pleasant, and very livable. I had two bedrooms, a living room, a small kitchen, and a balcony. I had no living room furniture and no TV. I did, however, have three beds. By Romanian standards, my apartment was quite roomy. For now, be it ever so humble, it was home, and it was just fine.

In the living room, a small white radiator — the only heat source — sat against one wall. There was an electric water heater (a purchase shared by Peace Corps and me) in the bathroom, so I had hot water. But only in the bathroom. The tiny two-burner hotplate in the kitchen was fueled by butane, and every time I cooked, I had to light the burners with matches. This cost me a few singed eyelashes at first, but eventually I got the hang of it.

I was actually quite fortunate. In some areas of Romania, it was common for the heat and the water to be turned off from 11 p.m. until 6:00 a.m. Romanians were just happy to have water, hot or cold. Period.

I loved going grocery shopping in Giurgiu. There were several little shops about a block from my apartment, including a dry goods store, a dairy, a bakery, and a butcher store. Meat and poultry could be purchased dead or alive, and I often saw an entire skinless cow, pig, or lamb hanging in the butcher shops. Chickens were often sold whole, as in complete feathered creatures with feet and a face.

Shopkeepers did not provide bags for your purchases, or anyone to bag your items for you. Everyone had his or her own *punga,* handy plastic or fabric bags brought from home. I kept one in my backpack at all times, along with my "Don't Mess with Texas Women" canvas bag.

On the streets, the old folks sold sunflower seeds wrapped in newspaper cones. For fresh veggies, I went to the open market and bought produce that had been picked fresh from the garden that morning. Milk, eggs, and homemade cheeses were plentiful. My favorite cheese was a luscious, indescribably smooth cheese made from sheep's milk. The availability of items in the market was totally dictated by the season. Although some imported fruits were available, they were expensive, beyond the reach of average Romanians, who had never even seen a banana or an orange under the communist regime.

* * *

A few weeks after I arrived in Giurgiu, I decided to change my cell phone service from a pre-paid, card-based option to a subscription service. The three young men working at the store were friendly and helpful. We chatted a little (in Romanenglish), and soon we were laughing a lot. I asked about the town and where to go to eat and get a beer. I was a novelty to them: friendly, curious, and very American. Most Romanians had never seen an American before, much less talked to one. Before long, we were eating peanuts and drinking beer, enjoying our own little happy hour right there in the store, all before noon. Eventually, we became good friends. I visited the store often, and the guys came to my apartment on several occasions.

When I first arrived in Romania, I imagined that I would see men that looked like Luca, the gorgeous Croatian doctor on NBC's *ER,* on every corner. That didn't happen, but I did spot a few who were indeed drop-dead gorgeous. Romanians are descendents of the ancient Romans and display a noticeably Latin character. The men are typically warm and spontaneous, small to medium in build, with dark hair, light skin, and a distinctive Eastern European nose.

But my point here is not how Romanian men looked, but rather how they behaved. Romanians totally embrace the practice of public displays of affection. Most of the PDAs I observed were heterosexual couples snuggling on park benches, but I also found the men to be quite open in their affection for each other, not in a sexual way, but rather as a genuine expression of friendship. I often saw boys and men enthusiastically embracing each other, and leaning affectionately on each other's shoulders in the Internet cafes, in a way that would make American men uncomfortable. But to me, it seemed a totally natural affirmation of friendship.

10
Failure to Launch (First Assignment)

Giurgiu, May 2002

> *My original assignment with Peace Corps Romania was with the Tourist/Environmental Club. In theory, environmental volunteers work with local community organizations in an effort to develop or expand environmental education and awareness. In retrospect, any similarity between my stated assignment and my actual experience was purely coincidental.*

From the beginning, my assignment was ambiguous and I was never exactly sure what I was expected to do. Since I had been assigned to an environmental program and the Tourist Club was not environmentally inclined, the project parameters were predictably muddy. Initially, the club wanted me to find funding sources so they could do "something environmental." They were not sure what that "something" was nor were they willing to set any goals. To them, I was just a cash cow. Unfortunately, the cash would never materialize.

In order to obtain the services of a Peace Corps Volunteer, an organization must first apply to, and be accepted by, the Peace Corps. The Tourist Club had originally presented itself as a bona fide organization with an office, a phone, and a staff — all the usual business accoutrements. It actually had none of these. When the Peace Corps checked out the club, they visited their "office" in the *Casa de Cultura*

(Culture Center) in Giurgiu to interview Ion, the director. It turned out that Ion worked at the Casa only as a guitar teacher.

In reality, the Tourist Club was a quasi environmental/musical group but they didn't do anything environmental. They did things musical. The club was composed entirely of a band and a singing group. They had requested a PCV hoping that, through the Peace Corps, they might get financial support or a little assistance with their programs, real or imaginary.

Undeterred by the misrepresentation, I decided to give the Tourist Club a chance. I would go camping with them the following weekend. (I was nothing if not flexible.) But you should know that my idea of camping is a hotel with no room service. My weekend trip with Ion and his Tourist Club to Campina, in the foothills of the Carpathian Mountains, would simply reaffirm this belief.

In Campina, I would sleep in a rustic, teepee-shaped cabin, I would frequent the now familiar Turkish toilets (the hole-in-the-ground variety with two convenient and totally useless foot rests), and I would long for a hot shower.

The occasion was a special gathering of Romanian clubs whose members professed to enjoy nature and the out-of-doors. What I actually observed was that they enjoyed singing outdoors, drinking outdoors, competing outdoors, and smoking outdoors. Communing with nature was low on the agenda. It may have been billed as an environmental thing, but no one was paying any attention to the environment.

Our tiny teepee was furnished with four (single-occupancy) camp cots that would have to accommodate the five of us: me, two teen-aged boys, and two girls, ages 12 and 16. The youngest girl ended up sleeping with the 18-year-old boy because she "didn't want to sleep with her sister." And no one, including Ion, seemed to care. I found this arrangement inappropriate in the extreme. Was this a Romanian thing? Later I asked several Romanian friends who had daughters if they would be comfortable sending their own child camping under these conditions. They said they would not.

We spent the weekend wandering through the early summer forest and "contesting"; we had poetry contests, singing contests, and racing contests. Fortified with plenty of beer and *tuica* and well into the spirit of things, liberally intoxicated men and women participated in the events alongside the children, who were left largely unsupervised. Ion wasn't around most of the time, stayed out late, drank too much, and slept till noon.

Most everyone seemed to have a good time.

Before we left on Sunday afternoon, I asked Ion about the trash, which covered the beautiful forested grounds. "The host club will clean it up," was his response.

Trash and litter are problems all over Romania. Everyone acknowledges the situation but no one takes any responsibility. I immediately wanted to implement a "Don't Mess with Texas" type of anti-litter campaign, and decided to contact a Romanian billboard company about donating unused space for the project. The company was willing to donate the space if we paid for the paper, but we never could find any donors.

Back home in Giurgiu, after a great deal of soul-searching, I decided to report my weekend observations to the Peace Corps office in Bucharest. I also discussed my concerns with Ion, who was quite upset by this perceived attack on his character. I had decided that unless Ion was willing to change his behavior — and the camp's sleeping arrangements — I could not continue to be a part of the group.

I was not the first PCV to express concern over the assignments of Group 14. My frustration escalated as more and more of the volunteers requested site changes. I was not yet at the point where I wanted to leave Giurgiu, but I really wanted to be involved in something long-term and productive. I made an appointment with Tina Covaci, my Peace Corps program director and my boss.

Tina was a passionate environmentalist who tempered her enthusiasm with humor and common sense. The first thing she would do when she came into her office on Monday mornings was turn on her computer and logon to my Web site. If I hadn't posted a new entry, she made sure I heard about it. Tina did not think my issues with Ion and his organization were out of line, and completely supported my position.

The Peace Corps does many things well — and a few not so well. In my opinion, they had not done a good job of screening the organizations to which my group was assigned. More than 20 percent of my group had asked for and received site and/or organization changes (usually a rare occurrence).

Shortly thereafter, in a fortuitous turn of events, the Peace Corps Office of the Inspector General visited the Peace Corps office in Bucharest. (Based in Washington, DC, the OIG reports directly to Congress on Peace Corps issues.) I was not one of those randomly selected to meet with the OIG. Instead, I had requested a meeting. I met with a very kind woman who, after listening to my story, told me this was not the first time she had heard of assignment difficulties from Group 14 volunteers. She also said something that both elevated and alleviated my frustration, "The Peace Corps has not been good to you." We both agreed that, based on my background, I should have been placed in a different sector, with a different organization.

A few weeks later, I was reassigned to the European Union Integration section of the mayor's office in Giurgiu. My new project looked promising. I would be working with Local Agenda 21, a United Nations-funded strategic planning project. Giurgiu was one of nine Romanian cities chosen to participate in this plan to help local governments develop strategies for sustainable development. This was the first time ordinary citizens had been asked to play an active role in Romania's economic recovery. They would do this by contributing input to a "local community agenda for the 21st Century."

In the beginning, I translated materials and correspondence into English. But as time went by, Adriana (my Romanian counterpart) and I decided that public relations and marketing projects would be a better fit. Finally, I was working in a field I actually knew something about, and where I might have a reasonable chance to contribute something useful.

11
Finding My Groove

Giurgiu, June 2002

We heard it constantly before we arrived and while we were in training, and it was in every PC manual. "Be flexible and have patience." I wear a rubber band on my wrist every day to remind me. I have been in Giurgiu a little over a month now, and in Romania for nearly four months. There are moments when two years seems like a lifetime, yet the days fly by. Life in the States is so comfortable and filled with such an excess of conveniences, but I am glad I am experiencing a life that is not. When I return home, I will appreciate what I have so much more. Mr. Whipple and Charmin never looked so good.

I've got wheels

One afternoon, I made a purchase that would change my life in Romania. I bought a bicycle. Being mobile opened up a whole new world. The bicycle was truly liberating, and I could now get across town lickety split. I could bring home more from the market in my basket, and packages from the States fit nicely on my rear cargo deck. Riding a bicycle also allowed me to explore parts of Giurgiu I might otherwise never have seen, and some I probably shouldn't have.

On a whim, I decided to cycle to the port of Giurgiu. The Danube River is spectacular here, as wide as the Mississippi and bustling with barges, sturdy tugboats, creaky ferries, and commercial ships plying the muddy waters. I admired the elegant buildings just across the river in Bulgaria, and the almost two-mile-long, double-decker Friendship Bridge that connects Giurgiu and Russe.

Although I was the only woman in the entire port, I never felt threatened, nor was I ever in any danger, this being essentially a country with almost no violent crime. Nevertheless, I always carried my cell phone with me. I struck up a conversation (in Romanian, of course) with an army officer toting a machine gun, who was defending the port (against what I'm not sure). Apparently his duties included sharing his lunch with the stray puppies that made their home at the port.

* * *

After months of doing the manual laundry thing, I bought a real, honest-to-goodness, life-changing washing machine. There were many to choose from, with all kinds of fancy buttons and cycles. I settled on a modest version with a brand name. I paid a little extra and had it delivered. Suddenly life got a little bit easier (and cleaner), not just for me, but also for Lourrae, who came over weekly to do her laundry. She bought the soap for both of us. However, I continued to dry my clothes on the balcony for all of Giurgiu to view.

My next significant purchase was not expensive, but it was difficult to find: a shower rod and a shower curtain. Romanian showers consist of large, wonderful bathtubs with hand-held showers — great when you want a nice relaxing bath, but a challenge when you need to wash your hair. The problem was keeping as much water as possible inside the tub, and sloshing as little as possible onto the bathroom floor. So I went on a mission and found not only a shower rod, but also a curtain and a support for my handheld shower. I could now take hands-free showers, and most of the water remained in the tub.

I have met the enemy and he bites
In June, the weather was marvelous with warm days and chilly nights. I still slept under a blanket and wore a jacket in the evenings.

It had also rained, which exacerbated the mosquito problem. Since I was living close to the river, the mosquitoes were many, mean, and thirsty, and there were no screens on the windows. Mosquitoes were everywhere, entire platoons of them. One evening, a Romanian friend came over and showed me how to put up screens the Romanian way. You cut a little netting, anchored it with thumbtacks and voila, you were set for the summer. Even so, the little critters still found their way in.

Every morning I doused myself with mosquito repellant. The stuff the Peace Corps had given us was army-issued and smelled terrible but worked great. My Romanian friends probably thought my American cologne very odd. I also bought a little electronic gadget highly recommended by the Romanians. You inserted little blue cards into the device, which emitted mosquito repellant and lasted about 10 hours. I wasn't winning the battle but the pernicious little bloodsuckers had a worthy adversary.

Day-tripping

One Saturday, Lourrae and I treated ourselves to a day in Bucharest. With a population of over 2 million, the city seemed a haven of modern luxury compared to Giurgiu. Once considered the Paris of the East, the city's wide boulevards and ornate architecture were originally modeled after nineteenth-century Paris, complete with its own version of the Arch of Triumph. Sadly, much of the city's historic center had been destroyed by Ceausescu's effort to design a civic center worthy of his reign. Many of the once grand buildings had lost their majesty, and the neighborhoods were overgrown with sterile concrete apartment blocs.

Our first stop was the Bucharest Mall (the only "Western" mall in Romania, built in 1999) with a tempting food court, a bowling alley, a 10-screen movie theater, a video arcade, and a parking lot with space for a thousand cars. In a country with so little money and so much need, the mall was a welcome surprise.

We walked around soaking up familiar sights, did some window-shopping, and saw a movie. It was glorious. Then we took a cab to an Indian restaurant recommended by some expatriate friends. We met the British owner who, since he was going in the same direction, offered to drive us to our next stop, my favorite Bucharest pub. A popular meeting place for English-speaking foreigners and young Romanians, the Harp was a great little Irish pub with good food and a comfy atmosphere. We spent the rest of the afternoon socializing with our new friends (two Aussies, two Scots, two Irishmen, and one Englishman).

* * *

In late June, my friend Liz invited me to spend two weeks working with ICAN (International Children's Advocacy Network) at an orphanage in Slobozia. Liz was a friend of a friend back in Texas, and was the medical officer for the Peace Corps in Latvia, Lithuania, and Estonia.

Slobozia is also home to the Slobozia South Fork, a Romanian version of the South Fork Ranch of *Dallas* TV fame. Hugely popular in Romania, *Dallas* was one of only a few American programs seen by Romanians during Ceausescu's regime. Although he was reportedly a fan, Ceausescu aired the series primarily to demonstrate the evils of Western capitalism. A combination tourist attraction and conference center, the South Fork didn't do as well in Slobozia as it did in Dallas, and it exists today as a silent, rundown imitation of American pop culture.

ICAN volunteers had been coming to Romania for more than 10 years to work in the orphanages; this was the fifth year for this particular orphanage. A popular Romanian artist was also part of the group. Using a kind of team effort (unusual in Romania), he had created a marvelous mural (the third one for the orphanage) on the outside of the building. He would first outline the mural in black, then show the team what colors to use to fill in the painting, sort of like an enormous paint-by-number picture. The support of a prominent artist in this beautification project helped to instill pride not only in the orphanage, but also in the community. Rather than being a place for throwaway kids, the orphanage had become an object of civic pride.

The orphanage was home to four groups of children: babies under a year old, toddlers under three years old, special-needs kids of all ages, and HIV kids, ages 11 to 16. The staff provided basic care for the children, but there were just not enough hands. ICAN had made a huge difference in the lives of these orphans, providing an extra measure of help, hope, and caring. They even managed to convince the head nurse that the "current" was not harmful, so the windows were opened wide during the hot summers.

After our work in Slobozia, I traveled by van with the ICAN volunteers for a brief visit to some of Romania's most spectacular sites — majestic mountains, flower-filled meadows, eighteenth-century Saxon towns, and mud volcanoes. A unique and rare geological phenomenon, the Mud Volcanoes of Bazau inhabit an eerie lunar-like landscape, where muddy chunks of earth simmer deep underground, then bubble upward, spewing out chocolate geysers and boiling pots of mud. It really was like a scene from another planet.

* * *

To strengthen our skills, Lourrae and I started private Romanian language lessons. We met twice a week at the home of a sweet lady who was an English teacher at the local junior high school. In addition to teaching and tutoring, Cami somehow managed to juggle housekeeping, mothering, studying, and looking smart and perfectly put together while also finishing her second degree at a university in Bucharest. Her husband, Paul, a customs agent and handy man, soon became our Mr. Fix-It. Whenever anything went wrong in our apartments, Paul would come over and make it right. We saw Cami twice a week and Paul almost as often.

* * *

Before I left Texas for Romania, a fellow Georgetown resident had called to tell me that her sister, the Rev. Mary Ferris, was in Romania as a mission co-worker in partnership with New Opportunities for Romanian Orphaned Children (NOROC), a non-profit Christian organization.

In June, I visited this amazing lady at an orphanage in Tulcea, an ancient city near the famed Danube Delta (Europe's largest wetland and a World Heritage Site).

NOROC provides for the orphans in material ways with things like diapers, school supplies, and shoes. But their most endearing effort is *Bunici Inmosi,* or "Big-Hearted Grannies," a program that ensures the caring personal relationships the children so desperately need. NOROC recruits these gentle grannies, mostly retired Romanian women, to make a positive difference in the lives of the littlest orphans. They work four hours a day, five days a week, giving individual attention and sensory therapy to babies and toddlers, and their efforts have made a profound difference. Orphanages that were once silent are now filled with the joyful sounds of happy children. The small salaries (about $1.25 per day) the grannies earn are an extra bonus, effectively doubling their pensions. If these women did not hold the babies, they would be left in their cribs most of the day. I wanted to take every child home with me, and I held most of them. Despite their circumstances, they were utterly appealing, needy, and full of life, and if they were not adopted (very unlikely), their prospects were bleak indeed.

NOROC also sponsors the Big-Hearted Teachers, which provides retired teachers to tutor students, and Big-Hearted Friends, which provides training, transitional employment, and housing for the older children, who must leave the orphanage once they reach the age of 18.

After visiting Mary in Tulcea, I felt that her Big-Hearted Granny Program was a story that needed to be told. Coincidentally, I discovered that a group of American journalists were holding a media symposium in Bucharest, and I was invited to meet them. I traveled to Bucharest to join them for dinner one evening at the Crown Plaza hotel, along with bureau chiefs and foreign correspondents from *USA TODAY, The Washington Post*, and others. One woman in particular impressed me. Rhonda Grayson was a reporter from CNN. Tall, stunning, and blond, she was also warm, kind, and interested in what I had to say.

I told Rhonda about Mary's program and two days later we were off to Tulcea to meet Mary and the grannies. But before we left Bucharest for Tulcea, Rhonda invited me to stay with her at her hotel. This was an invitation I could not refuse — unlimited *hot* running water, high thread-count cotton sheets, and the company of a compelling and caring person.

We quickly found a driver, a videographer, and a camera and forewarned Mary that we were coming so that she would not be surprised when we arrived with a reporter and cameraman in tow. Mary had to jump through hoops to get us into the orphanage, but we spent the day filming the grannies and playing with the kids. We met some of the original kids who had been "raised" by the grannies, and they were doing much better in their schools than the orphans who had not had the advantage of a granny's nurturing love.

Several weeks later, Rhonda's story aired on *CNN, Headline News,* and *CNN International.*

The ubiquitous maxi-taxi

Navigating the transportation system in Romania required something of a meteorological approach. I traveled most frequently by maxi-taxi (minivan) to Bucharest. In summer, the steamy weather had a significant impact on one's choice of transportation, and where one sat in the chosen transport. For example, if you boarded a maxi-taxi, you wanted to make sure you were NOT on the sunny side, a seat assignment that could cause you to end up poached upon arrival. A window seat was preferable, if the window opened. Even when the temperature was over 100 degrees, you encountered the dreaded "current" prejudice. If you did not have control of a window — and a buni (grandmother) did — you were toast. You could, and I did, sit in the front seat where you had both window control and legroom, but that seat also had its drawbacks. Maxi-taxi drivers drove fast and wild, like teenagers on the back roads of Texas. They could make your whole life flash in front of your eyes. They passed everything on the road — horses and wagons, cars and trucks — with impunity, often missing an 18-wheeler in the oncoming lane by mere inches.

The aisles were the worst. They usually filled up quickly with people traveling to the local villages, and there was always a chance that a reeking, intoxicated, garlicky old man would end up clinging precariously to a seat near me, his pungent aroma permeating the entire maxi-taxi. Whenever this happened, I fervently hoped that his stop was one of the first ones on the route.

Romania's favorite thug

Most Westerners are unaware that Romania was a very sophisticated society before communism tried to obliterate all things cultural and intellectual. In 2002, most homes still had hundreds of books, everything from science to literary classics. Cultural events were many and remarkable in most cities. Giurgiu had a popular theater and an impressive art gallery. Bucharest claimed world-renowned venues, among them the Romanian Athenaeum (home of the George Enescu Philharmonic Orchestra), the National Opera, the Caragiale National Theatre, and many, many museums.

Romania is also home to an abundance of public art, with parks and civic centers filled with beautiful fountains and sculptures of heroes, warriors, poets, and writers. Across from the mayor's office in Giurgiu is an imposing statue of Vlad Tepes, better known as Vlad the Impaler, the prince on whom Irish writer Bram Stoker's 1897 novel, Dracula, was loosely based. Depending on which side you are on, Vlad was either a beloved hero who fought to protect Romania from the Ottoman Turks, or an evil thug remembered for his extreme cruelty.

Stoker's blood-sucking vampire, Count Dracula, was a fictional character who lived in a sinister castle somewhere in central Romania, in the gloomy mists of Transylvania (which Stoker never actually visited). There was a real Dracula, but he was neither a vampire nor a count. His name was Vlad Tepes, and he was a fifteenth-century Wallachian prince known for his very unsportsmanlike practice of impaling traitors, petty criminals, and almost anyone else who annoyed him.

Vlad was famous for his gruesome methods of torture, which included skinning, decapitating, boiling, and burying his victims alive, but impalement was his favorite method of dispatching his victims (hence the title of Tepes, which means "impaler"). In 1460, 10,000 unlucky people reportedly ended up on the end of a stake in the city of Sibiu. The year before, on St. Bartholomew's Day, according to legend, Vlad skewered 30 thousand citizens in the city of Brasov.

Why did they call him Dracula? His father was called Vlad the Dragon because of his membership in the Order of the Dragon, a secret sect committed to preserving Christianity and protecting Wallachia from the Turks. The Romanian word for "dragon" is *drac,* so Vlad Senior was also known as Vlad Dracul. Vlad Junior became Dracula, the "son of Dracul." *Drac* also means "devil" in Romanian, and there were many who thought he was one.

Today, Dracula's legend still flourishes through tourist attractions such as Bran Castle in Brasov and the monastery at Snagov, where his headless body is reportedly buried.

Journey to the far side

In July, I traveled to Russe, Bulgaria, just across the Danube River from Giurgiu. Richard, a PCV in Russe, and I were working on a proposal for a cross-border project with the aim of increasing environmental awareness and encouraging more eco-friendly ways of life. The Russe-Giurgiu Environmental Education Project would send three groups of Romanian high school students to Bulgaria, and three groups of Bulgarian students to Romania, for environmental classes and cultural exchange. Participants would be chosen via an essay, written in English. Each group would take part in one program in Russe and one program in Giurgiu. The events would be timed to take place over a weekend, with the students arriving in the host country on Friday evening and returning to the home country on Sunday.

I was excited about this project. The governments of these two cities communicated with each other, but there was really no inclination for Romanians — or Bulgarians — to cross the bridge between the two countries. Part of the reason could have been the convoluted method of getting there. It took me two-and-a-half hours to go across the bridge (2.8 km) on a "slow" train, normally a 20-minute ride. And you could not buy a train ticket to Russe in Giurgiu. You had to go to Bucharest, 56 miles away — in the opposite direction.

Both host organizations were enthusiastic about the project, but since it would involve international travel, and all international travel had to be approved by Peace Corps country directors, the project never really got off the ground. The Peace Corps director in Bulgaria was very supportive, but the Peace Corps director in Romania was not. At the time, the Romanian PC director was a woman whose dubious decisions would eventually lead to her termination. Eighteen months into her tenure, she was asked to resign, too late to save our project.

* * *

I had been suffering from severe pain in my left heel, which was seriously compromising my activities, so I made a doctor's appointment at Peace Corps headquarters in Bucharest. Dr. Dan prescribed an anti-inflammatory but after two weeks, there was still no relief. An x-ray revealed that I had bone spurs on both heels, a situation that had been exacerbated by all my walking. Dr. Dan's advice? "Stay off your feet." We both laughed since this was not really an option. While I was there, Dr. Dan noticed a little freckle on my shoulder so I got the usual "stay out of the sun" lecture. Dr. Dan also suggested wearing long-sleeve shirts. I hoped he wasn't serious. It was 106 degrees that day.

That little freckle would later become a much bigger problem.

12
Bills, Bras, and Barnyard Animals

Giurgiu, June 2002
Independence Day is next week and I am sad I will not be
in the States. After 9-11, I am sure this will be an especially
emotional holiday. But the holiday will not go unnoticed by
me. I am currently living in a country where there were no
freedoms until only 13 years ago. I am lucky to have been born
in a country where my rights and freedoms are guaranteed.

Almost overnight, Romanian high summer was upon us. It was hot. Really hot. And it was only June. We had already had several straight days of temperatures well over 100°; one Sunday the thermometer outside my apartment registered 41°C (about 106°F). I drank gallons of water, wore as little as possible, and slept with cold packs that Julia had given me for therapeutic purposes. To avoid a total meltdown, I purchased some fans, which were really, really expensive, but really, really worth the investment.

Romania's bizarre hot-weather "policy" went something like this: If the "official" temperature reached 40°C (about 104°F), all work must stop and the employer must supply his employees with water. The problem was, the official temperature never seemed to rise above 39°C. It was, however, 40°C on a number of days. Just not officially.

The check is (never) in the mail

The concept of how money changed hands in Romania was fascinating, at least to my capitalist mentality. Checking accounts did not exist, and only about five percent of the population used credit cards. Even if you had a credit card, there were few places to use them. Bills were paid in cash, in person. To pay my electric bill, I first had to read the electric meter, then take the numbers to the city office, wait in line, and pay the bill. I paid my cell phone bill at the "bill" window at the bank, after waiting in line, of course. When I finally got a land-based phone line, I had to take the bill I received — in the mail — to the telephone company and pay the bill in person. Today, more and more people are using debit cards and cash accounts at banks. The last few months I lived in Romania, I was able to pay my phone bill at the ATM machine.

The bills for my water, *caldura* (radiator heat), and bloc fees were paid directly to the building administrator. The administrator added up all the water usage in my building and divided it by the number of residents. I then paid my portion. Those that could afford them installed water meters. This dramatically reduced your water bill since you paid only for the water you actually used. Those of us without a meter paid astronomically high water bills. Even when I was away, I still had to pay for water I did not use. Under communism, building administrators were hired not only to collect utility fees, but also to keep a watchful eye on the inhabitants. A file was dutifully kept on each apartment, and on the personal habits of each resident.

Summer style

In general, Romanian women could be divided into three basic groups: those who liked their bras to be noticed (majority), those who were more modest (minority), and those who did not wear a bra at all. The fashion trend at the time was to wear see-through (i.e., totally transparent) blouses, a trend that seemingly transcended age. And the key to being fashionable in your see-through blouse was to wear a contrasting lacy bra. If your blouse was white, you might wear a black bra. If your blouse was yellow, a blue bra would be fine, or if your blouse was black, the only color you could possibly wear was white. This attire was appropriate for office wear, general outings, parties, and major events. Surprisingly, the people I saw most often going braless were the older women, even the *bunis* (grannies), with their boobs resting comfortably at the waist. (I wasn't judging them; I just preferred not to be reminded of what I had to look forward to.)

Dinner on the hoof

You've heard the saying, "just like a chicken with its head cut off." I became all too familiar with the headless chicken thing by looking out my apartment window. Right before my eyes, I witnessed the preliminary stages of dinner preparation, a man and his chicken in a fight to the death. There was not much doubt about the outcome. The man was not gentle as he whipped the bird to the ground and chopped off its head with an axe. This was not the way I wanted to be reminded of my next chicken dinner.

Barnyard animals were a familiar site throughout both rural and urban Romania. I saw chickens on buses, rabbits on the subway, and I even heard about a horse on a train. One morning I saw an enormous muddy pig on a leash, headed toward the center of town. The most alarming thing about the pig was the hefty size of his testicles. I wondered how the pig could possible walk. I suppose it really didn't matter, since he was probably on his way to becoming someone's dinner.

Speaking of pigs, there is a popular dish in Romania called *slanina*, which is pork fat. Romanians like to eat it raw, right after the pig is killed. They also smoke it and eat it with a little mustard on special occasions. I have sampled this delicacy on two occasions, just to make sure I did not like it. It tastes a lot like the gristle on a steak.

Kitchen aids

Often during the sweltering summer, I would get a ridiculous urge to cook. Even when it was boiling hot outside, I hauled out the butane and fired up the cook top. One week alone, I made flour tortillas, apricot jam, cucumber soup, fresh-squeezed lemonade, vegetarian tacos (soy/wheat gluten is readily available and makes a great ground beef substitute), and a pitcher of banana smoothies.

One afternoon, I decided to have a go at making a Romanian specialty, eggplant salad. A succulent blend of eggplant, onion, and oil, it was not really a salad, but sort of a dip, meant to be served with slices of crusty bread. The trick was to char the eggplant first and quickly peel it before it assumed a burnt taste. Then you used a special wooden knife to cut up the eggplant since a metal knife would affect the taste. My first attempt turned out quite tasty.

* * *

For several months I had been watching some children who played under my window, just outside the building. One evening, I noticed two little fellows hanging around outside whistling. I stood in my window where they couldn't see me, and when they whistled, I imitated them. Startled at first, they looked around curiously, but they could not figure out where the "parrot" was hiding. After a while, they decided to fake a sneeze. I sneezed too and then began to laugh. Soon the boys were laughing with me. By this time a crowd had gathered, and I chatted with them through my window for a half an hour.

The next night I was working at my computer when I heard my name called. Several of the children had returned and wanted to visit. I quickly dug out the Texas pencils I had brought from home and headed outside. I met parents, siblings, aunts, and uncles, and soon had an invitation for dinner and a bicycle ride. I spent many summer nights with my new little friends.

While the neighborhood children were great fun and wonderful entertainment, there were other children whose plight was anything but. In almost every city I visited, I encountered the "puffers," ragged kids with empty eyes who walked around sniffing glue. Hoping to induce a chemical high, they would pour the glue in a plastic bag, cover their mouth and nose with the bag, and inhale the narcotic fumes. A few sniffs would temporarily numb the hunger and ache of poverty. Glue was readily available and cheap (about 50 cents), and many of the kids spent their meager funds on getting high rather than getting something to eat. Sadly, there seemed to be no effort to deter this unfortunate practice.

* * *

Cheap and available everywhere, flowers are a cherished part of everyday life in Romania. When I was invited to a Romanian colleague's home for lunch, Lourrae and I decided to bring flowers instead of wine or candy. We stopped at the flower market and looked for the vendor with the most beautiful blooms. We found her near the end of a long row, dressed like she had just come from her garden, a babushka wrapped around her head, an apron with large pockets (where she kept her money) tied around her ample waist, her calloused hands full of earthy evidence of her labors. She was selling magnificent bouquets of wild flowers that she had just picked that morning. It was almost noon and she was ready to go home, so she gave us five bundles for 20,000 lei (about 60 cents), cheap even for Romanians. Imported flowers are a little more expensive; a nice bouquet with paper and ribbon is about 100,000 lei, or $4. When you purchase flowers here, you always carry them upside down, with the blooms closest to the ground. I was told it was so the flowers "won't get stressed," but no one could really tell me the origin of this custom.

* * *

Most clothing sold in Giurgiu was cheap, as in poor quality. In order to get to a price that the Romanians could afford, costs had to be cut somewhere so quality was compromised. One wash and your new purchase could be history. There were many second-hand clothing stores, whose inventory was typically imported from Germany and other European countries. Second-hand stores were the *only* places you could find quality items at affordable prices.

And while I'm on the subject of shopping, the next time there's a sales tax issue in your town, consider Romania. In 2002, the national sales tax was a whopping 19 percent across the board. All services including phone, electricity, and water were taxed at that rate, along with property and income. There was also a "radio and television fee" added to your monthly electric bill. The fee was used to support the four state-run TV stations. You could avoid paying this fee if you could supply an affidavit stating that you did *not* own a TV or radio. You don't want to know how difficult these were to obtain.

13
Slobozia, Timisoara, and Baia Mare

Giurgiu, August 2002
Since my projects in Giurgiu have slowed a bit, I have accepted an invitation to visit several other Peace Corps programs in progress. I will travel first to Slobozia (by maxi-taxi), then to Timisoara via overnight train (no air conditioning, but it's much cooler at night). From there, I will take another train to Baia Mare, where I will help with a two-week English camp. I will be gone for nearly three weeks.

Slobozia

Gil (the PCV in Slobozia) had developed an innovative program that involved orphans helping orphans. As Romanian orphans age, they are moved to a more age-appropriate orphanage. When the babies outgrew the baby orphanage, they were moved to another facility, and so on, until they reach high-school age. Just a few blocks from the baby orphanage was an orphanage for high-school boys, many of whom had spent their early years in the baby orphanage. Gil had encouraged the older boys to volunteer their time at the baby orphanage, and now eight of them were making daily trips back to their old home to play with the babies. Watching a teenage boy playing with a baby is a remarkable (and often hilarious) sight, and I doubt if these boys had any idea of the valuable gift they were giving the babies.

83

Timisoara

After Slobozia, it was on to Timisoara near the Serbian border, where I would spend three days helping Community Habitat Finance (CHF), a U.S.-funded organization that works to improve conditions for disadvantaged people. Many of CHF's managers across the globe are former Peace Corps Volunteers. I had been invited to Timisoara to work on a public relations project to promote awareness of CHF's micro-loan program, which provided small businesses with a chance to grow their businesses. One example was a woman-owned business that was started with a micro-loan from CHF and was now a flourishing shoe store in Timisoara.

Timisoara was a lively, cosmopolitan city with a blend of Byzantine elegance and Western sensibilities. It was also the first European city to light its streets with electric lamps, and is home to Europe's oldest hydroelectric plant. The city was full of lush parks, charming fountains, trendy boutiques, and delightful cafes. The imposing Romanian Orthodox Cathedral, the scene of the first casualties of the 1989 revolution, anchors one end of the city center's broad flower-filled promenade.

As the story goes, the first victims of the revolution were a small group of children fleeing down Piata Victorie from Ceausescu's notorious secret police. They had hoped to find safety inside the church, but they would get no farther than the steps. The doors were locked, and the children were gunned down outside the front door. A plaque on the wall commemorates these young victims.

One night we dined at a Mexican-style restaurant called La Cucaracha. While the food was good, it was not Tex-Mex cuisine, which, of course, can only be found in Texas. And everybody knows that margaritas are made with limes, not lemons. Alas, limes were not available in Romania.

From Timisoara, I traveled north to Baia Mare for the English camp. At the train station, heading to buy bottled water for the seven-hour ride, I didn't notice the slope in the floor leading to a drainpipe. Wearing a travel backpack stuffed with three weeks' worth of belongings, I tripped, lost my balance, and fell. When I went down, the backpack pulled me over like a turtle on its back. Not a single soul came to my aid; that would not be the Romanian way. Everyone in the station just watched as I struggled to right the turtle.

Nightmare on the Baia Mare Express

On the train to Baia Mare I shared a compartment with a pleasant, attractive Italian gentleman. Even with my limited Romanian and his imperfect English, we had a most enjoyable conversation (I think). At one point, my new friend even jumped off the train and bought us both a beer. He got off the train in Satu Mare, about an hour from my destination.

As the train rolled on toward Baia Mare, I pulled out my book and began to read. A few minutes later, the conductor — a disheveled, dark-haired man in his mid-30s — entered the compartment and sat down beside me. Odd, I thought, since every other seat was empty. After a few unsuccessful attempts to engage me in conversation, he decided to try another tack. He leaned over and began to touch my breasts, rubbing his hairy hands slowly across my shirt. In Romanian, he told me to "lie down and I will give you a massage." Ironically, it was the first time I had ever bought a first-class ticket. I was an American woman traveling alone. This would never have happened to a Romanian. And unless I was missing something, I was pretty sure a massage was not included in the ticket price.

Angrily I asked him to move to the seat across from me. Then I noticed his wedding ring and tried to distract him with questions about his family. There was no one else in the compartment and I was not brave enough to scream FUCK OFF. Whatever I tried to do, he could overpower me. Finally, after no, no, and NO, he left.

I decided to move to another compartment so I would not be alone. Horrified, I realized I was the only passenger in the entire car. After a short while, back he came with a smirk and a qualifier, "I'm sure you will like my massage." I was frightened the first time, terrified the second time. I knew I was alone. He knew I was alone.

After what seemed like an eternity, but was probably only about five minutes, he left. I immediately used my cell phone to text-message my friends in Baia Mare, asking them to meet me at the station.

When the train finally arrived in Baia Mare, my Peace Corps pals were all there on the platform. We trooped into the train station, and when, a few minutes later, my assailant walked in, I yelled THAT'S HIM. The police substation was just inside the train station, so we immediately headed there. If you are thinking clean, official, well-organized, policies in place to protect the people, this was not the case. The policeman I talked to was not even in uniform. He kept referring to some sort of law book, obviously very old. Apparently, he was not at all familiar with the law he was supposed to uphold.

As soon as I could, I called the Peace Corps emergency line, which was available 24/7/365. Dr. Dan (a Romanian) was on the line right away. About the same time, one of the other volunteers identified the perpetrator to the policeman, who immediately walked him into a small room next to ours, presumably for questioning (and I hoped, indictment and hanging).

Over the phone, Dr. Dan talked first to the policeman, then to the assailant, the interpreter, and the other volunteers. Suddenly attitudes began to change. The policeman donned a uniform, the perpetrator became a puddle, and I quit shaking.

Names were taken, statements made, and after two hours, we were finally free to leave. As we headed out the door, one of my friends said to the policeman, "I think we all need some polinca" (a twice-distilled homemade plum brandy, strong stuff at 150 proof). The policeman just happened to have some in his file cabinet (much more useful than a law book).

Baia Mare

Shortly after I settled in at my host volunteer's apartment, he announced that about 150 kids were expected to attend the English camp. (My host was also a Group 14 PCV, assigned to Baia Mare.) Although English was taught in most Romanian schools, the English camps provided a popular venue for children to practice their English skills, important if they were to be able to access the global information provided by the Internet and other media, most of which was in English. For many Romanians, learning to speak English well could also lead to a better job.

For me, summer camp has always evoked memories of fun activities, campfire songs, and the requisite camp apparel. Not this camp. Since the camp was being held at a school, none of the kids wore shorts. In Romania, children do not wear shorts to school, so they came dressed in school clothes — long pants, nice shirts, skirts for the girls. The school venue was also probably the reason the kids were so formal, raising their hands to speak and standing at the side of their desk when speaking.

But this was a camp, and the kids were supposed to have fun, so Carrie (another PCV) and I decided to trade the formality for some frivolity. First we pushed the desks to the back of the room so all that was left were the chairs, which we arranged in a circle. Next we let the kids come up with some rules, and we added a few caveats such as "no need to raise hands to speak or stand by your desk when speaking. Just be respectful of others."

Each day I helped with the arts-and-crafts activities, some days for more than 50 kids. When I checked the supplies, which were almost nothing, I wondered how we could possibly manage to entertain so many kids, but I needn't have worried. In Romanian schools, children have no opportunity for art or cultural activities, so even though we only had one pair of scissors, most of the markers were dry, and there never seemed to be enough paper or glue, it didn't matter. I was amazed every day at the wonderful pieces of art these kids created, making something out of almost nothing. Literally.

The last day of camp we played games. I brought a Bop-It game and Carrie fabricated a Twister game on the floor. The kids had a great time. It had nothing to do with learning English, and everything to do with having fun.

14
Horseradish Is a Root

Giurgiu, August 2002
  One afternoon, I came home from work and discovered that the phone service in my apartment building was not working. Romtelecom, the state-run telephone company, could not explain the problem nor were they particularly interested in fixing it. They did not work on weekends or past three in the afternoon, and the customer was definitely not a priority. It took them nearly a week to locate the problem and even longer to make the necessary repairs. A year ago, this would have been extremely frustrating. But I had adjusted. I did as any Romanian would do. Who needs a phone?

Pickling things

I love horseradish on my roast beef and gefilte fish but beyond buying it off the shelf in the refrigerated section of a supermarket, I knew nothing about it. Until I came to Romania.

For whatever reason, I made a conscience decision to learn to make pickles. I felt that if I were successful at pickling cucumbers, I might venture into pickling other veggies for the long winter ahead. I studied the recipes in my Peace Corps-issued cookbook for both summer pickles (quick pick) and winter pickles (take longer, last longer). I decided that I would do both since they shared some of the same ingredients.

89

One of the ingredients required for winter pickles was fresh horseradish. Since I didn't know what fresh horseradish looked like or where it came from, I wasn't at all sure what to look for in the market. Before I ventured out on my quest, I practiced saying "horseradish" in Romanian. There was no sense looking stupid on both accounts. I also wrote the word down on a piece of paper just in case I got tongue-tied. Did you know that horseradish is a root, and fresh horseradish looks like a stick? I eventually found it in the market but it took a few visits. I almost bought what looked like white carrots before I was redirected to the correct vendor (I still don't know what the white carrots were). I was very pleased to have successfully negotiated this purchase, which cost me all of 3,000 lei or around 9 cents for a bunch.

When I got home, I peeled my new purchase and it smelled so good I thought I would give it a little taste. If you've ever gotten that burning feeling in your nose when you've eaten too much processed horseradish — well, go with that and multiply it by a hundred. It was head-blown-off hot. I made three large jars of pickles, one summer and two winter.

You have a package

Unless you were visiting an establishment with Western ties, such as McDonalds, Pizza Hut, or KFC, customer service, as we Americans know it, was virtually nonexistent. Take the post office for example. A package sent from the States could take anywhere from one to six weeks to reach Romania. And once it arrived at the post office, it could sit there for several more weeks before the postal worker or customs agent sent you a notice.

To pick up your package, you had to go to the central post office and stand in line. Even if you got in line very early in the morning, there was no guarantee you would be able to pick up your package that day. And even if the customs agents arrived late, they never stayed past noon, no matter how long the line. Those still waiting simply returned the next time the external package office was open. Initially this cavalier attitude caused me to think homicidal thoughts, but I needed only to look at the rubber band I wore on my wrist to remind myself of my Peace Corps mantra: Be flexible. (And bring a book.)

I received many wonderful and welcome packages from home while I was in Romania. Whether it was food, smelly girl stuff, or cooking utensils, these packages were a comforting connection to home. It was always exhilarating whenever I got a notice in my mailbox that I had a package. Usually I had to wait a few days to pick it up, since international package pickup in Giurgiu was only available on Tuesdays and Fridays. Some of the items I received were a huge surprise; others were things from my "list." Either way it was always like Christmas, Thanksgiving, my birthday, and warm fuzzies — all in one package.

I'm sure I was the only PCV with a year's supply of Charmin toilet tissue, which made me supremely happy and the envy of all. I was also the only PCV with a stovetop popcorn popper (6 quarts in just 3 minutes) and it made the best popcorn ever. There were also sparkly pens and pencils, lots of magazines, and wonderfully fragrant girl stuff. Tuna (in water) was the most essential item I received and probably the only protein I ate for months, besides cheese. Whenever I traveled to places where I knew I would be seeing other volunteers, I always took along something to share. The lounge at PC headquarters was buzzing when I brought in the Oreos. Things that didn't last long: beef jerky, Rice Krispie Treats, Jelly Bellies, Life cereal, and of course, Oreos.

* * *

Although most Romanians worked in offices that were not air-conditioned, I did not. That's the thing about mayor's offices: Cooler heads are needed to prevail. Romanians like to get to know you before they trust you enough to work with you, so I went to lots of meetings. It was the Romanian way. And at every meeting, no matter how warm the weather, I was offered coffee and cookies. Since I didn't drink coffee, I had to eat the cookies. If I didn't, it would have been considered rude.

Every day I looked forward to lunch at the mayor's office. We would gather together, spread out our lunches, and share and socialize. Being included made me feel more like a part of the group and less like the American volunteer. We usually ate Romanian lunchables like tomatoes, peppers, cheese, bread, paté, and ham. Occasionally I would make something totally American to share, which helped dispel their perceptions of (bad) American food.

My favorite Romanian lunch was fish egg salad (which tastes better than it sounds). One of the girls made it really fresh; she bought the fish alive from the market and harvested the eggs at home. I shared a few of my American recipes and my co-workers were amazed that the ingredients could be found right there in Giurgiu. Tuna salad was the favorite. My Romanian friends had never thought of adding pickles, onions, and mayo (which most Romanians made themselves). One day I brought tamale pie. It was the talk of the office.

One Sunday, I went to one of my favorite vegetable stands to buy tomatoes. I bought a kilo and then asked the vendor about his watermelons. I wanted a small one so he tapped and thumped until he found the perfect melon for me. He would not let me pay for the melon. I came back two days later to buy more tomatoes and told my new friend how good the watermelon was. He gave me another one.

This was not the first time this had happened. The lady who sold me the hand-carved wooden utensils always gave me a little utensil whenever I bought a big one, the dill man gave me an extra pepper, and the flower lady gave me two bouquets for the price of one. I like a bargain as much as the next person, but these people had so little and yet they were so eager to share. Maybe it was because I was an American, maybe it was because I amused them when I stumbled over words, but it was inspiring to know these gentle, generous people.

One afternoon I went to my little shop for some butter. Suddenly, my eyes were drawn to a shelf that held *sliced white bread.* In Romania, bread usually comes in a loaf that looks like French bread. Nothing sliced about it. I splurged and bought the bread for 18,000 lei, or about 55 cents (regular Romanian bread costs about 9 cents). For lunch that day, I invited Lourrae over for home-style French toast and syrup, which I had to make since they don't have syrup in Romania. The greatest thing since sliced bread is still sliced bread.

* * *

Riding my bicycle through the streets of Giurgiu was thrilling — and could be a near-death experience. According to the Peace Corps Handbook, I was supposed to wear a helmet whenever I rode my bike. There were, of course, no helmets in Romania. The Peace Corps had ordered some, which were due to arrive in October, but this was August and I doubted if the Romanian drivers would wait that long to run me over. Sometimes drivers got so close to me their side mirrors grazed my arms. My friend at the mayor's office told me to get the license numbers of the offenders and they would take care of it. I was not exactly sure what that meant, so I never took him up on the offer.

15
You Can't Get There from Here

Giurgiu, September 2002
  The moon was full while I was at the Black Sea, the moonrise
  golden and breathtaking. Knowing it was the same moon
  that my friends and family back home were seeing made the
  world feel like a smaller place.

Laura, a bouncy, energetic brunette fresh out of college, was the PCV assigned to Campina, just north of Ploiesti. She came to visit me one Saturday on her way to see friends in Russe, across the river in Bulgaria. It took about 30 minutes to show Laura all the sites in Giurgiu, including the fountain and our enchanting eighteenth-century clock tower built during the Turkish occupation. Like most small towns in Romania, Giurgiu was charming and quaint, and the people wonderful, but it was, well, small.

One of the high points of Laura's visit was our Kraft Macaroni & Cheese lunch at my apartment. After lunch, we did something I had wanted to do ever since I moved to Giurgiu. We went out for a beer. There were lots of places that sold beer in Giurgiu, but none would have been appropriate for a single woman to visit. So Laura and I went to a restaurant (going into a bar would have been scandalous) that had a nice, cozy terrace and drank a beer apiece. It was cold, and it was good.

When it was time for Laura to catch her train to Russe, we headed for the station. From my previous experience traveling to Russe, I knew you could not purchase a ticket to Russe in Giurgiu. You had to go to Bucharest. When I had traveled to Russe before, I had had help negotiating the ticket purchase, but we would have no help his time. Nevertheless, two heads were surely better than one, and together, we could speak twice as much Romanian. How hard could this be?

We decided to use my bike to get to the station. There are two train stations in Giurgiu. The central station handles domestic trains; the station we needed was in the far northern part of town and was used only for international trains.

Laura rode on the back of the bike on the cargo deck, and I did the pedaling. Getting started was the hard part, but once we were rolling, it was nothing short of exhilarating. My heart pounded as we whizzed past four policemen; in Giurgiu, it was against the law to have a passenger on the cargo deck. The policemen yelled something in Romanian that I did not understand, and we cycled on.

At the station, they told us what we already knew: You could not buy a ticket from Giurgiu to Russe. "You must go to Bucharest." And in Bucharest, they tell you that cannot buy a ticket in Bucharest for Giurgiu-Russe. You must buy it in Giurgiu. This seemed totally absurd. The Romanians were equally frustrated with the situation. There obviously was not a big demand to travel across the river to a town we could see from our window. So we decided to think like Romanians. We would bribe the conductor.

About this time, an older gentleman appeared. He had been working in his garden near the station and saw me cycle by with Laura in tow. We explained our dilemma. He told us what to do and how much to pay the conductor. Laura and I also chatted with the customs officials just to be sure all the right people were happy. Fifteen minutes later, everyone was in agreement that Laura could board the train without a ticket. I waited until the train pulled away from the station, just in case. I never did find out how much she actually had to pay the conductor.

My new friend then invited me to inspect his vegetable garden. I unlocked my bike and he pushed it the hundred meters to his garden, which was huge and filled with wonderful vegetables. Dressed in baggy pants and a worn sweater and covered with proof of his agricultural skills, he proudly explained that he grew everything organically. Then he picked some herbs for me to smell, all the while describing what dishes they would taste best in. He told me all of this in Romanian, so I understood only half of what he said. He showed me all the potatoes he was storing for the winter, explaining that, although he had only planted about five kilos, he was harvesting much more. We picked fat carrots, dug up potatoes, cut parsley and celery root, pulled plump tomatoes off the vines, and selected some juicy grapes. His small garden produced more than enough vegetables for his family, his children, and his grandchildren, and he was happy to share his good fortune. In my heart, he had planted a seed of kindness I would not forget.

Life's a beach

As the days grew shorter, I found myself traveling in a steamy, crowded maxi-taxi back to Mangalia on the Black Sea for a little fun and some in-service training (IST). The mornings were filled with language lessons, but each afternoon we headed to the beach, where I soon discovered it is only we Americans who are intimidated by our bodies. In Romania, it didn't matter how old you were or what shape you were in. Beach attire seemed to transcend age, and included two-piece, one-piece, and no-piece swim suits. Every man on the beach who was not a PCV was wearing a Speedo. The women wore Speedos or thongs, and only about half of them wore any tops. Females of all ages — from teenagers to grannies — bared their breasts and bottoms. This shocked no one but the Americans. Romanians are comfortable with who they are, and they don't pay much attention to bodies, theirs or anyone else's. All the same, I always wore my wind shorts over my bathing suit whenever I went to the beach.

From Mangalia, I did a little sightseeing, then hopped a train to Sinaia for our Technical IST. Tucked away amid snow-topped mountains, Sinaia was once the home of shepherds and hermits, later transformed into an aristocratic retreat. Today the town is a popular vacation destination and ski resort. Sinaia is also home to Peles Castle, a spectacular confection in the Bavarian-Renaissance style, considered one of the most beautiful castles in Europe. Built between 1873 and 1883 for Romania's imported German monarch, Carol I, the castle had been decorated by his slightly eccentric wife and consort, Elizabeth (also known as the popular novelist, Carmen Sylva). The castle has over 700 magnificent stained-glass windows, and its 160 rooms are lavishly decorated in mother-of-pearl, marble, walnut, ebony, and ivory, and are filled with exquisite artifacts, medieval weapons, Murano chandeliers, and one of the most valuable art collections in Europe. Peles was the first European castle with electric lighting and central heat, and the first to sport a built-in electric vacuum cleaning system.

During Ceausescu's reign, the castle was appropriated as a private state retreat, although Ceausescu did not like it much and seldom visited. Nevertheless, the dictator hosted numerous world leaders in its splendid rooms, including U.S. presidents Richard Nixon and Gerald Ford.

While I was at Sinaia, I learned about a remarkable environmental education project for junior-high school students. Developed by PCVs, the program was already being used with much success in Cluj, a city in the Transylvania region of Romania. I was immediately interested. This was something that was definitely doable and could have a significant impact in Giurgiu. I decided to take the curriculum home, study it, and try to find a way to put it into practice.

Bribery in the classroom

Education in Romania was compulsory until age 16, and transportation to school was almost never provided. In remote villages, students as young as six often walked up to four miles to school if there was no public transportation. In general, there was no school lunch, since school either ended before lunch or started after lunch. And in 2002, teachers still smoked in the classrooms and religious icons were obvious and numerous.

Grades were extremely important, and often determined which high school you attended, increasing (or decreasing) your opportunity to get into a university. The practice of buying academic grades was often used to ensure acceptable exam scores and to gain admission to schools and colleges, and graduates often had to pay even more bribes just to get a job. Teachers also paid bribes to guarantee promotions or profitable transfers. In 2002, new teachers were earning about 1.8 million lei a month (around $55), which was probably why they felt the need to supplement their income. I heard a credible story about a teacher who was given a washing machine. All the kids whose parents contributed to the purchase of this machine were given stellar grades.

Most Romanians speak at least two languages, often more. They study more subjects than we do in the States, and there are virtually no extra-curricular activities. But in spite of all the emphasis on education, lack of suitable employment was (and still is) a continuing source of disillusionment and frustration for most young Romanians. The major occupation for most people was the daily struggle to put food on the table and keep a roof over their heads. They expected little and were seldom disappointed. But unlike many affluent nations, poverty did not automatically mean unhappiness to Romanians.

End-of-summer party

August had almost burned itself out. On many warm, muggy evenings, the neighborhood children stood below my window, calling to me to come out and play. Grubby, giggly, and precocious, these kids were curious about the redheaded American lady who was their neighbor. I played with them as often as possible, and when they figured out which door was mine, they came knocking.

One afternoon I had a sudden inspiration. I would have an end-of-summer "craft" party. As I mentioned before, Romanian children did not receive any type of art instruction in school. Since many schools didn't even have phones or running water, art was not a priority. I had some craft supplies I had received from the States and Lourrae, an avid beader, brought over her beads. We fixed some snacks, organized our crafts, and we were set. The kids decorated balloons, made collages, strung beads, giggled at my Romanian, and learned new English words. When the last kid left, I knew we had created magic, not because of the cake and punch or even the crafts, but because they had allowed us to be their friends.

A room with a view

The next weekend I moved to a new apartment. My old bloc was a 30-minute walk from the center of town. In my new flat, everything would be five minutes away. The major reason for my relocation, however, was the fact that my apartment had no stove, only the butane cooktop. The landlord had promised one, but the stove had never appeared.

After I decided to move, I set out to find a suitable place. I bought all three of the local newspapers, scoured the classifieds, and finally found an apartment that sounded promising. I set up a meeting with the landlord to take a look, and shortly thereafter, it was a done deal, all negotiated in Romanian (even I was amazed). Some Romanian friends with a van helped me load my belongings and transport them to my new abode. I was surprised how much stuff I had accumulated in a few short months; my possessions had morphed from three suitcases into about 20 hefty boxes.

My new apartment was smaller but cozier. You entered through a small hallway with doors that opened to a living room, kitchen, bedroom, and bath. Red-and-black carpeting pieced together like a puzzle covered the concrete floor in the hall. The living room was decked out in purple carpeting with some bookshelves, two chairs, and a foldout couch. The bedroom was half the size of an average bedroom in the U.S., but roomy enough for another foldout, more bookshelves, a desk, and more red-and-black carpeting. I had a working stove, hot water (in the bathroom), and most important, heat. I was living large on the eleventh floor of the tallest building in Giurgiu, with a wonderful view of most of the town and some of Bulgaria, just across the river.

* * *

In late October, the weather turned cold. The heat in the building would not be turned on until there had been three consecutive days of temperatures below 50°F. So far, it had not gotten that cold, but a smoky haze had begun to settle over the city in the evenings. Many of the older houses still used wood-burning *sobas,* large, floor-to-ceiling ceramic heaters fueled by wood. The *sobas* were actually beautiful, often made from hand-painted tiles, and the smoke they produced left a sooty, surreal fog hanging over the city, perfuming the air with the sweet, familiar scent of autumn.

I had been warned that in January the snow could get as deep as I was tall (5'2") but January was still three months away. One morning toward the end of October, I woke up to a sparkling sea of white. The park below my window, the rooftops, and the streets were all covered in a beautiful blanket of snow. I couldn't wait to bundle up and make my trek to the office. My Romanian friends thought I was crazy but I explained that I was from Texas and we didn't get much snow, and when we did, everything usually shut down.

Giurgiu did not shut down. In fact, there was even more activity in the streets the morning after the snowfall. The ladies who picked up the street trash every morning were now the official snow shovelers and the streets were cleared by 7:00 a.m., the sidewalks by noon. I wore my snow boots to work, carefully navigating the potholes and ankle-deep slush at the intersections. I was charmed by this first snow, a feeling that would quickly dissolve when the snow became a daily inconvenience.

The cold weather also introduced a new fashion statement. The Russians did at least one thing right. They invented those wonderfully warm, furry Cossack hats that work great on both men and women. I did not see the hats much on young people, but the older crowd wore them like crowns.

* * *

Meanwhile, I was still dealing with painful heel spurs. Resting and staying off my feet were at the top of the list of recommended therapies, but this was not possible in my line of work. Despite 12 days of laser therapy at a clinic in Bucharest, my feet were as painful as ever. So I hopped a maxi-taxi to Bucharest and went back to Dr. Dan for the next course of action: the "boot," a cumbersome plastic device I wore at night for two months. Designed to keep the heel stretched out while you slept, the boot also failed to resolve the problem. So I soldiered on, swallowing the pain along with the ibuprofen.

Me and Lourrae (my site mate) in front of the hub.

The language class (in front of the elementary school where we had classes).

Dana, my host mother during training.

Buni.

One of the jewels of Romania's historical sites, Peles Castle.

Dana's apartment building in Ploiesti.   *Bran Castle.*

View from my 11th floor apartment in the springtime and during the winter.

My pride and joy, my English Club, at our last meeting, March 2004.

Christmas party at Speranta, organized by the English club girls.

English camp in Baia Mare.

Traditional costumes at a dance festival for the harvest in Giurgiu.

Danut's family.

Anca, the little orphan who underwent heart surgery.

Training the teachers at a junior high in Giurgiu. January 2003.

CNN's Rhonda Grayson, visiting the "Grannies of the Heart" program at the orphanage in Tulcea.

The Danube Delta, one of Europe's largest natural wetlands.

Dinner with the Cazacus during my mother's visit, April 2002. (This was the first time I met Mrs. Cazacu.) From left, Tata Andrei, Mama Zoica, me, Andrei, Carol Peterson (my mom), Costin (Andrei's brother).

The Cazacu family when Tata Andrei was a little boy. From left, Nitisor Cazacu (priest and father), Matei (brother), Mona (standing), Georgeta (mother), and Tata Andrei.

Canopy of flowers at our Romanian wedding, Valentine's Day 2004.

Cutting the cake at our second wedding in Georgetown.

16
Rain Showers and Champagne Toasts

Bucharest, November 23, 2002
   *Being an American is a blessed thing. We have been given
   the gift of freedom, a gift that does not come easily to much
   of the world.*

On November 23, President George W. Bush made a four-hour visit to Romania to officially welcome the country into NATO. All Peace Corps Volunteers were invited to the event, which hosted hundreds of thousands of jubilant Romanians packed shoulder to shoulder in *Piata Revolutiei* (Revolution Square). If I had known we would be standing in a cold rain with thousands of people for six hours waiting to hear the U.S. President speak, I probably would have declined the invitation. But this was history in the making for my Romanian friends, so I was happy to endure the elements.

About 300,000 people crowded into the square, possibly the largest crowd Bush addressed during his presidency. Accompanied by his wife Laura, Colin Powell, Condoleezza Rice, and Ari Fleischer, President Bush was joined by the Romanian president and a number of Romanian celebrities, including Nadia Comaneci (1976 Olympic legend and a hero in Romania), Ilie Nastase (remember the historic 1972 U.S. Open against Arthur Ashe?), and Georghe Hagi, the soccer great who put Romania on the map at the 1994 World Cup. As we waited in the chilly rain, we were entertained by music from some of Romania's top bands.

109

Revolution Square was a fitting venue for this historic event. Just 13 years earlier, in the same square, Nicolae Ceaucescu had given his last speech, the last gasp of his despotic rule. Bullet-riddled buildings were still in evidence, silent reminders of the heroic Romanians who lost their lives in the fight for freedom. Behind the National Library, the former Securitate headquarters stood in ruins, witness to the horror of the former regime.

The square was decorated with American, Romanian, and NATO flags, and spectators were given tiny, soggy Romanian and U.S. flags to wave. Banners and chants proclaiming WE LOVE USA, THANK YOU USA, ROMANIA-USA, and NATO NATO NATO filled the square. Security was clearly visible. We were searched and patted down and had to pass through two security stations. I even had to open both my lipsticks for the security agents, one a lovely shade of red, the other a ravishing gloss. Snipers carrying big guns stood on the tops of the surrounding buildings, eyeing the crowd through binoculars.

There was another reason for the significance of the U.S. presence in Romania that day. I had been told on more than one occasion that the Romanians had waited and waited after WWII for the Americans to liberate them. The older generation sadly recalled parents who had waited until they died, thinking America was coming to save them from the tyranny of communism. One elderly gentleman told me that, although his own parents were dead, his mother in-law was thrilled that the Americans were finally here. She had waited nearly 60 years.

Another perspective

Romanian President Ion Iliescu opened the festivities. As he was speaking, a rainbow arced across the sky above the square. President Bush waved delightedly to the crowd, giving them a thumbs-up and remarking on the favorable omen and the munificence of God's blessings. There was nothing presidential about his behavior. It might have been a touching moment, but President Iliescu was still speaking. When Iliescu finished his speech, President Bush took the podium. He spoke about freedom, about the historical significance of Romania's NATO membership, and made many references to the Iraq situation and terrorism (the topics of the day). Bush was much more presidential during his speech, which included the following message:

The path of freedom you've chosen is not easy, but it's the only path worth taking. I know that your hardship did not end with your oppression. America respects your labor, your patience, your daily determination to find a better life. Your effort has been recognized by an offer to NATO membership. We welcome Romania into NATO.

At the end of the day, most Romanians saw the event as a catalyst for economic change, an opportunity for Romania to finally move forward. The day was charged with emotion and full of promise, and I was glad to have been a part of history, proud to be an American, and filled with hope for Romania's future.

* * *

The week of my birthday, I loved checking my e-mail; there was always a special new greeting. Several friends and family members even called, a real treat considering the cost of this type of sentiment. On my birthday, Lourrae and I went out for dinner. This was the first time since arriving in Giurgiu that I had actually gone to a restaurant for dinner. There were several nice restaurants in Giurgiu but Romanians typically did not spend money dining out, reserving such extravagance for only the most special of occasions. It was also very expensive. We chose an Italian restaurant. We hoped to see pizza on the menu and it was — and so much more. I ordered the ravioli and was not disappointed.

I was tempted to let my birthday pass quietly, but my Romanian friends insisted that I have a party. In Romania, the tradition is to throw yourself a party, so that's what I did. I made enough food, Romanian and American, to feed an army. The concept of "dip" was unknown to my new friends and it took awhile to find the correct words to explain it. I finally described it as a sauce for chips and veggies. I found a round loaf of bread, made a bread bowl, and filled it with spinach dip. The Romanians caught on quickly and ate every bite.

My guests sang the Romanian birthday song and showered me with champagne, literally. There was a nice mix of people, young and old, students and professionals, and of course, Lourrae. We danced in my tiny living room until well past midnight. I also got bunches of text messages (on my cell phone) from other volunteers. Cheaper than calling, texting is the major reason you have a cell phone here. In fact, Romanians were texting on their cell phones long before it ever became popular in the U.S.

Little things mean a lot

All my life, I have craved order and structure. I make lists whenever I go to the market, I cannot leave the house until it is straight, and I often spend more time organizing than doing. I recognize that this need for order is my way of feeling in control of a sometimes chaotic environment, and this ordering of my small universe is a huge comfort.

I knew that, in moving to Romania, I would have to give up many things. But one thing that I could not give up was my habit of washing my face every day with a clean, white washcloth. There is something very comforting to me about this little ritual, so I made sure I included a good supply of washcloths in my "essential" luggage. A friend in the States even sent me addition cloths in one of my birthday packages.

One Sunday morning I woke up and instinctively decided I would go out and get the Sunday paper, crawl back in bed, and read it cover to cover. It took me a second to realize — with huge disappointment — that there were no Sunday papers here, and I was not in Texas. I missed the comfort of familiar habits. A few months later, a friend sent me a Sunday paper in a care package, which I read in bed, cover to cover like all Sunday papers should be, relishing the months-old news and advertisements.

One of my birthday packages contained two little bits of heaven, a butter-soft flannel nightgown (I could be sexy in flannel, right?) and a beautiful Wedgwood-blue sweater. Both had those little plastic things that attach the price tag to the garment. I had not seen one since I left the States, but there was something comforting in its familiarity.

I had brought a few scarves with me to Romania, which I used to add a little character to my limited wardrobe. I kept the scarves in a quilted satin envelope that belonged to my mother. I loved opening the drawer with the satin envelope and seeing something I had been looking at my entire life.

The joys of not blending

No one would ever use the term "wallflower" to describe me. All my life I've attracted attention, whether I wanted it or not. As a child, it was because I had bright orange hair. As I got older, it was because of my boisterous laugh. Now, as an American living in Romania, it was because I was so obviously a foreigner. People stared in blatant and disturbing curiosity (normal in many foreign countries). They were not being rude, just expressing an honest and unabashed interest. At first it didn't bother me, but after I had been in Romania for almost eight months, it started to drive me nuts. Because of my heel spur problem, I wore tennis shoes regularly, almost unheard of in Romania unless you are a child. With my red hair, hard-to-ignore laugh, American dress-up clothes, and white sneakers (lace-up hiking snow boots in winter), there was no way I was ever going to "blend." Not even close. But once I uttered a few words of Romanian, suspicions were replaced with genuine interest and the inevitable questions, "Why are you in Romania? What is life like in America?"

If you were Romanian and you were with an American, the attention escalated. I asked my language tutor if we could spend some time in the market so I could learn the names of some of the items about which I was totally clueless. We spent a lot of time in the meat alleys, I with notebook and pencil, writing down all the new words. The customers and the butchers probably thought we were some kind of inspectors, and if that was the case, I hoped I would at least get a fresh cut of meat. I didn't.

17
Madame Director

Giurgiu, December 2002
Decades of communism have left Romanians with a deep-rooted culture of corruption, fear of change, and an inherent distrust of others. From customs officers and gravediggers to high-ranking officials, professors, even doctors, everyone expects a kickback. Surprisingly, most Romanians do not find this practice strange. Ordinary citizens expect to ante up cash in order to get quality services, or any services at all.

The Peace Corps requires every volunteer to have a secondary project. Since October, I had been meeting with people from the Department for the Protection of Children (DPC), the Romanian agency that manages all state orphanages. I wanted to offer my services as a volunteer. I might as well have tried to offer my services as an astronaut. In navigating the murky waters of Romanian bureaucracy, I would be swamped by the notorious bribery, incompetence, and apathy, before I would ever succeed.

The first week in December, I met with a lovely woman who was the deputy director of the organization. I explained that I was interested in volunteering in an orphanage. She told me that I would have to meet with her boss, the director of DPC.

The next week I went back and met with Madame Director, an unpleasant, mousy-haired, middle-aged woman who was just plain mean. Pleasantries were not exchanged. My typical demeanor usually involves smiling and gushing. Madame preferred scowling and huffing. I explained what I wanted to do. Madame replied, "Can you bring me money?" This was said a number of different ways, a number of different times. I got the picture. If I wanted to work in the orphanage, I would have to give her money.

With her menacing manner and no-way mentality, Madame was a classic example of communist-inspired bureaucracy at its finest. And she was not about to bend, not for me, not for the orphans, not for the greater good. For cash, however, she probably would have even smiled.

Madame requested some literature about the Peace Corps and asked me to come back the following week. I came back. She kept me waiting for two hours and then said she could not see me. This was not an uncommon practice in Romania. Keeping someone waiting demonstrated that you had power and authority, and Madame had elevated this practice to an art form.

I persisted. I pleaded. I turned up regularly like a bad penny. I reminded myself that the goal was to benefit the kids. I went back four more times over a period of about two weeks. Each time, I was dismissed after waiting several hours in a chilly common room used by the social workers. I spent much of the time conversing with a pleasant Romanian woman who had lived in Canada and spoke excellent English. I learned that she was the wife of a Romanian doctor, and although she and her husband had found jobs at a Canadian hospital, her husband had not been allowed to work as a doctor. They had returned to Romania because her husband missed practicing medicine, and she had subsequently found employment with the DPC. I was grateful for her small gesture of friendship in the otherwise alien abyss of Romanian bureaucracy.

On the fourth visit, I was finally granted an audience with Madame, who told me my request would have to wait until after the Christmas holidays because she was very busy. All she really had to do was say yes. There were no papers to fill out, no application to submit, no authorization required. The only thing keeping me from working in the orphanage was Madame, and she was not interested in any seasonal charity. As kindly as I could, I explained that I had a two-week holiday coming up that I could spend working with the children. But I had not produced what she wanted (cash), so I was not going to get what I wanted.

Frustrated but not defeated, I did some sleuthing and found out that, in fact, Giurgiu County runs the local orphanages. In October, I had met the Giurgiu County Prefecture at an international trade show in Bucharest. He was a kindly gentleman in a powerful position and most superior to Madame. He had even suggested that I call on him. It was time to make that call. I arranged a meeting and he did not keep me waiting.

The Prefecture had no authority over Madame, but he made a call to the President of the County Council, who did. The next morning, I went to his office to plead my case. He made one phone call to Madame. The following day, I was playing with the kids. Madame may have lost this battle, but she would eventually win the war.

* * *

I spent the week before Christmas at St. Andrew's. Housed in a moldering old brick building, the orphanage was home to about 70 children in four groups: newborns, infants, toddlers, and the sick children in the infirmary. The rooms were institutional in appearance, with white cement walls and tile floors. The floors in the common rooms were covered with green indoor/outdoor carpeting, which was the only color in the room. The toddlers' common room had a small, blue vinyl padded area, which was used like a playpen, and the disabled children were often left there for hours. There were few toys and limited recreational or educational activities. The children slept in rows of white metal cribs next to the common area. Everything happened on schedule: The kids had breakfast in their cribs, then they were rinsed, changed, and dressed. Heavy cloth diapers covered their bottoms unless guests were present, in which case the disposable diapers were used.

The children suffered from visible neglect and a lack of any caring, emotional connections. There were no hugs, no smiles, no nursery rhymes or bedtime stories. The staff pushed food into little mouths at mealtime, stoically observed the kids while they were in the common room, and otherwise offered no signs of interest. A few seemed to care about the children, but they were the exception. In their defense however, there were only one or two workers for every 10 kids, and they were obviously overwhelmed by the daunting task of caring for 70 children. By the time it was playtime, the staff members probably felt they deserved a rest.

Behavior and lack of attention and affection seemed to be the biggest problems, the latter probably the cause of the former. The kids bit, hit, screamed, and threw tantrums. They would rip toys out of each other's hands and scream when they didn't get what they wanted. It might have been age-appropriate behavior, but the lack of attention and discipline had exacerbated the problem, and the children acted more like animals than human beings.

I spent the first week observing and playing with the kids. I crawled around on the floor and let the kids tumble all over me. There were lots of laughs and hugs. This kind of interaction had probably never happened in their entire short lives. Meanwhile, the staff sat on straight-backed chairs and watched with disdain and disbelief.

One day, I was left alone with the kids. This gave me a chance to see if any of my child-guidance skills would work. I was familiar with the concept of timeouts, so I decided to create a *sala pentru plange,* or "place for crying," in a corner. The words were mine — and probably meaningless to a Romanian. If a toy was taken from a child, I gave it back. If the child who took the toy screamed, so be it. I had a special place where they could go to scream and let off steam.

At least half the children got to experience the *sala pentru plange.* They would stay about 30 seconds, stop crying, get a hug, and come back to play (sort of a timeout without a timer). With one little girl, eventually all I had to say was *sala pentru* and she would stop crying. These were baby steps, but even more astonishing, the staff was beginning to use timeouts with the children.

There were no miracle behavioral changes, but the kids began to listen and to respond to me. I continued to use the practices that worked, hoping the staff would see that the effort paid off. As the kids began to trust me, I tried to spend a little one-on-one time with each child. They had no toys except for a few pages torn from books. Financially, the orphanage had trouble just feeding the kids. Toys were simply not important. Over time, the kids came to consider me a sort of big, floppy, redheaded toy. I often thought how blessed we are in the United States, with so many resources to deal with social problems and people's misfortunes.

In 2002, conditions in the state orphanages were still appalling, and the problem of unwanted children persisted. Access to education and birth control was extremely limited and birth rates remained high, while family incomes were pitifully inadequate. But relief agencies are beginning to concentrate their efforts on family planning and long-term solutions, and some orphanages have been replaced with smaller, family-type group homes.

18
'Twas the Night Before Christmas, and the PigsWere Nervous

Giurgiu, December 23, 2002

I'm sure it is because I am the "American," but I've received many invitations to attend parties and concerts this week. I turned down none of them. School Seven had a variety show, the religious school had a Christmas concert, and the music school had a recital. These performances were more casual than those in the States, but the parental pride was exactly the same. I also attended the mayor's Christmas party and danced my first Romanian folk dance.

Under Ceausescu, Christmas was never celebrated openly. December 25th was just another workday. Today, Romanians celebrate Christmas in much the same way as many people around the world. They decorate their homes, bake cakes, exchange Christmas cards, and trim their tiny Christmas trees. Children wait anxiously for Santa Claus (*Mos Craciun*, or Father Christmas) to leave small gifts for everyone under the tree.

A few days before Christmas, the traditional pig is slaughtered and magically transformed into all manner of goodies including roasts, sausages, and various other charcuterie like *toba* (intestine stuffed with meat jelly) and *slanina*. Every single part of the pig is eaten, including the skin.

121

When I was in Romania, the fatted Christmas pig was traditionally killed by slitting its throat. Because of European Union standards for the ethical treatment of animals, many Romanians fear that such ancient practices will have to stop once the country is admitted to the EU. There were rumors that the pigs might have to be killed by pistol or electrical shock to avoid the animal's suffering. However, since traditional methods are deeply ingrained, and most Romanians don't have a gun, the Christmas pig might indeed live happily ever after. *(Note: Romania was admitted into the EU on January 1, 2007. The fate of the Christmas pig is still uncertain.)*

Carols are also a very important part of Romanian Christmas festivities. Two days before Christmas, the children set out through the neighborhood, caroling from door to door. They are rewarded with traditional treats like fresh pretzels *(covrigi)*, candies, apples, and money. The pretzels are homemade and delicious, found at special booths in the market during the Christmas season. Quite a few carolers visited my apartment and the songs were beautiful, the young voices pure and full of holiday cheer.

Many homes had small "Charlie Brown" Christmas trees, very festive with a few ornaments and some tinsel. Some hung up Christmas wreathes, but the decorations were simple and understated.

I spent most of my first Christmas in Romania eating. The day before Christmas, I ate a delicious dinner at Cami's house. Afterward, I went to the orphanage to play with the kids. On Christmas morning, I was back at St. Andrew's. The director was stunned. In the States, people are often involved in helping others, but in Romania, this is not a normal practice. I hoped to lead by example; the kids would come first, not the holiday.

On Christmas Day, a very sweet lady (a teacher at the school where I was doing my eco-ed training) picked me up and took me to her home for yet another holiday feast. And the day after Christmas, I maxi-taxied to Bucharest for one more festive dinner with a lovely lady I had met in, of all places, a maxi-taxi. Mihaila spoke excellent English and was thrilled to meet an American. After our initial meeting, we had chatted on the phone several times and she insisted I come for a holiday visit. While I was at her home, I felt like some kind of prize on display; all her friends and neighbors dropped in during the afternoon to meet me and watch me eat. It was a wonderful dinner, so I did not mind being the entertainment.

My Christmas feasts were largely traditional fare, beginning with cold meats, fresh cheeses, and olives, followed by jellied pork, vegetables, and a sour soup. The main course was usually *sarmale cu mamaliga* (stuffed cabbage rolls with polenta). Dessert was a mouth-watering selection of pastries and *cozonac,* an old-world, holiday sweet bread filled with walnuts or raisins and seasoned with cinnamon. During the meal in Bucharest, everyone gushed as they watched me eat, especially when I bit into the jellied meat. They told me I had just eaten the best part, the pig's ear. I never ate jellied meat again.

New Year's miracles

The week after Christmas, I visited St. Andrew's almost every day, spending most of my time trying to get the kids to connect with each other. We rolled a ball on the ground, danced to some folk music, and sat in a circle listening to a story. I wasn't a complete failure, but it took lots of patience and perseverance to work with kids who were so afraid that the hug you gave them that morning might never repeat itself.

Playing ball turned into a competition to see who could get into my lap, and books were simply items to be torn apart. But dancing was a gift. After some initial struggles and a huge leap of faith, I managed to get four of the children to hold hands and dance around in a circle. We did this for about ten minutes, an eternity for kids so young. I was elated and the staff was astonished.

I was beginning to find an answer to the question, "What am I doing here?"

After the dancing, I thought I would push the envelope a bit with ring-around-the-rosy. I didn't know the Romanian translation, so I tried it in English with three little girls. We rang-around for what seemed like ages, and my thighs were killing me from all the ups and downs. They did not need to understand the words; they just enjoyed the rhymes and after one or two turns, knew exactly when to fall down. Little miracles.

Most of the younger kids took a nap about mid-morning. This meant they were put in their cribs and left until lunch, crying and howling. Nothing would rouse a staff member to go to them or try to calm them.

A few of the little ones had spent so much time in their cribs that the backs of their heads were flat and their legs bowed.

On New Year's Day, I was back at St. Andrew's. At naptime, five of the older kids were put in the room with the little ones, and all of them were howling. They had a lot to cry about, but some of the crying was just to make noise. Finally I couldn't take it anymore, so I decided to sing. I could think of only one song and I sang it over and over and over: "Amazing Grace." As I sang, I rubbed a little back or tummy. After about 30 minutes, all was quite. For today anyway, they each had a little peace. *La Multi Ani!* Happy New Year!

Romania is a seriously cold place in winter

The temperature had not risen above freezing for weeks and it had been snowing for days; in places, the drifts were thigh-high. Two months earlier, when it snowed for the first time, I had taken lots of pictures and reveled in the magic. It was all wonderful as long as it lasted only a few days. But now it had snowed so much that just walking in town was treacherous. I wore my snow boots every day, but indoors I wore my fluffy leopard slippers. Fashion still counted. And my woolen socks were the best things that had happened to my feet since my first pedicure. I wore layers and layers of warm clothing, and I never saw my skin in winter.

For most of January, the days were gray, raw, and bone chilling. Cold permeated everything. The heat in my apartment came from three elderly radiators, which had to be "aspirated" every day to remove air from the pipes. I would open the faucet on the end of the radiator, hold a bucket underneath, and drain about ten buckets of water from EACH radiator. There was no ON and no OFF. When the heat did work, it was ON all the time. When the heat was not working, the temperature in my apartment hovered around 58°F. Whenever this happened, I would pray, on my knees, that the heat would be fixed before dark, when nightfall brought a precipitous drop in temperature.

The first winter in Giurgiu, I did not take showers because the wind whipped through my bathroom at gale force, making a shower too cold, even with hot water. All the bathrooms in the building vented into a shaft that ran from the ground floor up to the roof. If I stood on the bathtub, I could see into the next apartment. I finally figured out that if I stuffed plastic bags into the vent, I could block off the cold air, and gain the occasional luxury of a hot (okay, warm) shower.

Along with snow and cold, there was also lots of ice. The first time I fell on the ice, I was visiting Peace Corps friends in Galati and we were headed out to a movie. I hadn't taken three steps before I collapsed to my knees on the ice. After that, my friends and I hooked arms to ensure I did not fall again. But in Giurgiu, I was on my own. I watched the bunis carefully because they didn't fall very often; in fact, I was actually rescued by a granny the first time I fell. I noticed that they took small, shuffling steps on the ice, and walked on the far left or right of the sidewalk where there was more snow and less ice. I tried their method and it helped.

The sewer children

Dressed in ragged clothes and often shoeless, thousands of homeless children, some as young as six, escaped Bucharest's brutal winters by living in the city's squalid, rat-infested sewers. A vast, underground network of tunnels containing steam pipes (no sewage), the sewers were constructed during Ceausescu's regime to provide apartment blocs with heat. But the pipes lost most of their heat underground, so the sewers were toasty-warm instead of the apartments.

Whenever I visited Bucharest, I would often see these street children begging for food. Those who had visited their subterranean "homes" reported a surreal world with no natural light, tiny candles flickering on walls, and an overwhelming stench. In their dank, underground world, the kids would warm soup over stubby candles, some sniffing paint thinner from paper bags to numb the hunger. It was warm in the sewers, and the kids had nowhere else to go.

Poverty and circumstance have forced these children to seek refuge wherever they can find it, surviving by begging, stealing, and occasional charity. Some of the children were runaways from state orphanages, which were notoriously short on food and compassion. Some had escaped abusive homes or had left home because their families could not support them. Some were children of the original children found living in the sewers when the communist government toppled in 1989.

The sewer network was not Bucharest's only underground communist souvenir. The city's infamous, secret tunnels are lingering reminders of

Ceausescu's supreme conceit. In the 1980s, while the city was starving, the tunnels were reportedly filled with all manner of food, clothing, and supplies. The tunnels were a part of Ceausescu's fail-safe plan. In case of attack, the regime meant to survive there for a very long time.

Romanian writer and National Public Radio commentator Andrei Codrescu reported on the rumors surrounding the Bucharest tunnels in his memoir, *The Hole in the Flag*:

> *The metro entrance gaped at our feet like a huge open mouth. We had read that the metro entrances of Bucharest were also entry points into Ceausescu's maze of tunnels, a secret subterranean network constructed to outlast even nuclear war. There were reports of rooms stocked full of canned and frozen delicacies, armories containing missiles, communications centers gleaming with the latest technology. The underground network was reputed to be thousands of miles long, multilayered, a complicated nervous system whose exact shape and direction no one single person knew. Architects who had worked on portions of the system had been killed.*

When I was in Romania, an estimated 20,000 homeless children lived on the streets.

19
Carpe Every Diem

Giurgiu, January 2003

My first year in Romania is almost over, and, although I don't look different, I am changed. So much has happened over the last few weeks, both good and bad. Unfortunately, I can't pick up the phone and call home, or cry on Julia's shoulder, or call up Julie in Houston to share my special moments. My emotions get all bottled up inside and so I write, which for me is like screwing the top off of a shaken Coke bottle. It is liberating.

The environmental education program I first learned about back in September at in-service training was finally getting off the ground in Giurgiu. My plan was to implement the program in all fifth- through eighth-grade levels. I would first train the teachers, then train the trainers, using a flexible curriculum designed to work at any classroom level. But before anything could happen, I needed the blessing of the vice-mayor and the school superintendent.

As luck would have it, coincidence and politics were on my side. In just a few years, the Romanian government would be requiring all schools to implement environmental programs, and the program I was proposing would not only meet these requirements, but would also cost the school district nothing.

In spite of what seemed to me to be obvious benefits, the superintendent did not immediately embrace my proposal. He was in fact, downright suspicious, especially since I wanted nothing in return. But after three arduous meetings and much review of the curriculum, he finally gave his approval. From the time I had first pitched my idea to the vice mayor until we had our first training session, four months had passed. But this was "Romanian" time so things had actually moved pretty quickly.

The program was based on a new interactive teaching methodology, very different from the highly structured classroom instruction found in Romanian schools. It took courage for the superintendent to see the possibilities, and to realize that good things could come from this new way of teaching.

Before we could begin the training, we needed instructional materials, so I asked the vice-mayor for help in printing a few teaching manuals (which had already been researched, written, and translated into Romanian by PCVs). He generously agreed, and soon we had 400 books to give to the school district. I sent out press releases for the first training session, and the Giurgiu newspaper and the local TV station covered the event. Even the vice-mayor came. It was a huge public relations coup, demonstrating that the city not only endorsed, but also wholeheartedly supported the program.

The first teacher training session was held at a local junior high school. About 25 teachers attended, and 15 students were invited to help demonstrate the first lesson, which was a "game" designed to demonstrate the relationship among all the elements of an ecosystem. For example, a student would toss a ball of string to the next student to establish the "connection" between, say, plants and water. By the end of the game, the room resembled a giant spider web.

First, I taught the lesson to the students. Then it was the teachers' turn. In Romania, teachers typically stand in front of a class and lecture, expecting the students to listen quietly and memorize all the salient facts. Then they test. It is all very structured and definitely not interactive. It also does not allow for any analytical or creative thinking. This new method — using games and props — was completely alien to the Romanian educators. Initially, many of the older teachers had difficulty buying into the new program, but they eventually came around. This was, after all, fun stuff.

I began each training session with an icebreaker, something that's never done in Romania. I would start with something like "My name is Lisa, and I had yogurt for breakfast," or "My favorite food is Joe." (Joes are scrumptious wafers with hazelnut cream inside.) I'm sure they thought I was a little crazy, but it worked. Although most of the students understood English, many teachers did not, so we always had a translator.

In the Peace Corps, the goal is to train your counterparts so they can continue your work after your service ends. To that end, we were enormously successful, eventually training more than 200 teachers.

Invisible children

Most of the thousands of Romanian children living with HIV/AIDS endured heartless and widespread discrimination, which often kept them from attending school or receiving even basic medical care. By refusing to acknowledge them, the government could pretend they did not exist. Many of these children had become infected from vaccinations or blood transfusions, commonly used at the time to treat anemia and malnutrition.

Lourrae's primary Peace Corps assignment was with Licurici (firefly), a Romanian organization for HIV/AIDS children and their families. Earlier, I had helped the organization with several projects, and now they had asked me to teach basic computer skills (e-mail, Internet, word processing, etc.) to mothers of HIV children. I scoured the Internet for resources I could use to provide a beginner's course for these women who had so little and desperately needed help and hope.

Over several months, we met each week using three computers: my laptop, Lourrae's laptop, and one aging computer that belonged to Licurici. The women giggled, struggled, and learned, eventually acquiring valuable skills and a heightened sense of pride and self-worth. Today, the little organization is a highly effective community resource with several computers, mostly acquired through grant writing done on their original computer. Thanks to recent awareness campaigns and organizations like Licurici, Romania's surviving HIV children are no longer invisible, and most can expect to live normal, productive lives.

* * *

In early January, I learned that a little three-year-old girl from St. Andrew's was desperately in need of heart surgery. Anca was born with an atrial septal defect (a hole in the heart) and needed an operation to correct the defect. I did not understand why she had not received medical attention earlier, but I managed to get a copy of her medical file, which I shared with a Romanian friend who was a cardiovascular surgeon. He made all the arrangements, and Anca was operated on the last week in January.

In preparation for her surgery, Anca spent a week in the hospital undergoing tests, which would have taken a day or two in the States. Most of the time, she was free to play. A Romanian hospital, however, is vastly different from a hospital in the States. It is a serious place and can be quite scary for a child. Think drab, cold, sterile, and unfriendly. I spent several days with Anca at the hospital and killed at least 20 roaches every day. It got to be a game.

Although the Romanian doctors were excellent and the staff was kind and helpful, medicine is practiced differently in Romania than in most Western countries. Money is always an issue. While Ceausescu was in power, no new medical practices or equipment were allowed into the country. After the revolution in 1989, Romania had to play catch-up, and the country didn't have the money to make up for so many lost years very quickly. I heard about a brand-new echocardiograph machine in a Bucharest clinic that went unused because no one knew how to operate it.

Anca's surgery was a huge success, and she is living happily ever after. Shortly after her surgery, she was adopted by a Romanian family.

Seeds are sown

In late January, I started working with a 10th-grade civics class at one of the local high schools. The class was participating in a USAID (U.S. Agency for International Development) project to promote volunteerism in Romania. The kids were asked to suggest and implement a project, and I was invited to participate in a discussion where the kids would be presenting their ideas. Apparently, the local press had been told about the American who was working with the class, and that I would be giving a speech that afternoon. I learned all this after I had arrived and was sitting comfortably in my seat in the auditorium. Welcome to Romania! It all turned out fine, and the student's ideas were great.

A few days later, one of the girls called me with her "plan," which was to work in an orphanage. I sent her to Mariana at St. Andrew's, who referred her to Madame, who summarily turned her down (no surprise). She ended up volunteering her services somewhere else. Other student projects included collecting trash in a park and mentoring kids. These were the same ideas I had put forth initially, but it didn't really matter where the seeds had come from. They had been planted. _

In America, the concept of volunteerism is deeply rooted in our culture. When we are given the opportunity to help one another, we do. We contribute to our churches, buy Girl Scout cookies, volunteer at soup kitchens, or coach little league. In Romania, volunteerism is extremely suspect, and is never encouraged. Whenever I saw a single Romanian helping another, I was immensely hopeful.

Hell freezes over

I had been told that this winter was the harshest in recent years. It certainly was the harshest one I had ever experienced. Snow was a constant, and ice covered the ground for weeks at a time. By the time the roads and sidewalks were cleared, it would snow and sleet all over again. Maybe it looked like a winter wonderland, but it really was hell frozen over.

Early one morning I headed to the orphanage after an overnight snowfall. I decided to take a taxi instead of tackling the snowdrifts on foot. I waited and shivered at the taxi stand for a long time, watching my breath curl in the air while the snow fell around me. Eventually a taxi came, but the drive to the orphanage was slow going. I was beginning to think that I should have stayed at home with a good book, but it was too late to change my mind. The taxi couldn't take me all the way to St. Andrew's, so I got out a few blocks from the orphanage and walked the rest of the way in knee-deep snow. When it was time to leave, I slogged my way home — two long, cold miles — through the drifts.

The dirty uncles

Marco and Paolo were Italian businessmen and also my next-door neighbors. They worked with "old" iron, of which there was an infinite supply in Romania. They would buy the iron, ship it to a storage area where it was all smashed up, and then loaded onto boats for sale to other countries.

I called them the "dirty uncles" because they were both married, with wives in Tuscany, girlfriends in Romania, and an endless supply of cash in Giurgiu. They were also friendly and very generous. When I needed Christmas presents for the orphans, they gave me several hundred dollars to buy gifts. I often socialized with them, watched TV with their girlfriends, and shared food and wine. Marco and Paolo simply made things more interesting. Marco spoke very little English and resembled a benign little grandpa. Paolo was about 40 years old, charming, and very Italian. He spoke decent English and had a four-year old daughter back in Livorno.

Marco and Paolo were familiar with my ongoing non-negotiations with the DPC. Now that I was onboard as a volunteer at St. Andrew's, I had decided that the orphanage could really benefit from multiple volunteers. The orphans desperately needed the attention, and I had found a group of young people who wanted to help. It all made sense to my American mind.

The Young Democrats were a group of young Romanians affiliated with PCD, the political party then in power (similar to our Young Republicans). I had met them at St. Andrew's during the holidays when they brought gifts and fruit for the kids, so I knew they were interested in helping the orphans.

Several weeks earlier, I had presented my proposal for the multiple-volunteer program to the Commission of the DPC. Although they were not the same group I had worked with initially, they proved to be just as formidable. You would have thought I was trying to import nuclear weapons (actually, that would have been easier). They interrogated me for several hours and when I left, I felt like a common criminal. They concluded that I was probably a spy from the Western press, secretly planning to bring ABC back to report on the continuing atrocities in Romanian orphanages. DPC was apparently still smarting from ABC's 1992 exposé on Ceausescu's orphans, "the starving, hollow-eyed children kept in cribs for years."

The DPC remained intractable and suspicious of my motives. They did not understand why I would leave my country to work in Romania

— for free. I wasn't making any money, I wasn't stealing babies, so they believed I must have an ulterior motive. In any case, my efforts had seriously stalled, and I was beginning to feel like a hamster on a wheel.

I explained my frustrations to the dirty uncles. They offered to set up a meeting with their well-connected friend in Bucharest, who had helped them negotiate the requisite bribes and mindless bureaucracy associated with doing business in Romania.

Recharged by their offer of help, I suggested that I meet with their friend the following week in Bucharest at McDonald's, home of Big Macs, saturated fats, and clean bathrooms.

The dirty uncles were about to change my life forever.

20
Legal Aid

Giurgiu, February 2003
  Sometimes you reach a point in your life when you come to
  the conclusion that love has passed you by and that your
  life is meant for other things. I knew that working with the
  environmental program and the kids at the orphanage was
  where I wanted to be. And I was certain I would go back
  home at the end of my service with an adopted child. But
  sometimes, just when you think you are headed down the
  right path, you come to a fork in the road and must choose
  between the unknown and the familiar.

The following week, on a bitterly cold Friday morning, I set out for Bucharest to meet with Andrei Cazacu Sr., recruited by the dirty uncles to help me in my efforts to establish a volunteer program at the orphanage. Mr. Cazacu spoke no English and had asked his son, Andrei Jr., a Bucharest lawyer, to provide translation services for our meeting. Unexcited about his father's request and not very confident of his own English skills, Andrei had reluctantly agreed to come. "If this young lady can leave her home and family in America to help the Romanian people," he would at least make the effort. Andrei told his father to go ahead, and he would shave, shower, and join him at McDonald's as soon as he could.

McDonald's was conveniently located in an underground metro station, so it was easy to get to. I arrived a few minutes early. Mr. Cazacu arrived a few minutes later. The dirty uncles had given me a few clues to help me recognize him: distinguished-looking, medium height, balding, thick square glasses. I introduced myself in Romanian, and we talked a little about my situation. He attempted to explain that his son would be coming soon to interpret.

About 30 minutes later, breathless and sweating in spite of the cold, in swept the son, Andrei, looking quite smart in a double-breasted blue blazer, white shirt, tie, and wool overcoat. Initially, I wasn't that impressed. I couldn't figure out why he was so nervous, avoiding eye contact and grabbing napkins to wipe the sweat that was streaming down his face in rivulets. He would become much more appealing as the hours passed.

My meeting may have been with the senior Cazacu, but it was Andrei, with his shy smile and flying napkins who got my attention. He was bashful, suddenly charming, and totally embarrassed. Most of all, he seemed to have a big soul. We connected immediately, ordered some beer (yes, beer at McDonald's), and the meeting stretched on for several hours. Conversation drifted from talk about the orphanage to talk about one another, and eventually a plan was devised. The Cazacus would come to Giurgiu to help sort out my orphan problems.

Note: In this section, Andrei's voice appears in italics.

When I arrived at McDonald's, I immediately saw my father sitting at a booth with this very attractive redheaded American woman. Right away, I liked Lisa and felt comfortable, not so ashamed of my English. My father noticed how much we talked and excused himself often to make phone calls (smoke breaks). Lisa laughed a lot and I admired her for what she was trying to do. I knew it would not be easy but I liked her optimism. We in Romania are not so optimistic.

Until that moment at McDonald's, my perception of American women had been based almost entirely on American television shows and movies imported to Romania. Although Lisa was very determined, she also seemed kind and caring. And, unlike many women on American

TV, she was not armed. I wanted very much to see her again so I told her I would call.

The next morning, I was like a lion in a cage. Over coffee in the kitchen, my father teased me, "You didn't even want to come to McDonald's." Throughout the morning, I weighed my options while sweating and pacing the floor. I really wanted to see her again. I wanted to call her, but maybe I shouldn't. She might say yes. She might say no. She might not even answer the phone. I continued to pace and sweat. I was pacing so much I could have dug a ditch. Finally my father said, "What's the worst thing that can happen? If she says no, the world won't stop, the air will still be there."

I decided to end my agony. I picked up the phone and called. She said yes.

Anxious that all would go well on our first date, I decided that Club A, a Bucharest institution and a favorite of university students, would be the perfect venue. Club A had been a part of my life ever since I started going to clubs and was considered a popular haven for free speech and intellectual debate, even during communism. In the 1970s and 1980s, the club was the genesis of some of Romania's most popular bands. But in spite of its colorful history, it wasn't very impressive, just a tiny little place in an old section of Bucharest with cheap drinks, great music, and lots of energy. I hoped Lisa would like it.

I did not invite Andrei to pick me up. Instead we agreed to meet back at McDonald's and go from there. McDonald's had been lucky for us before, it might be again. Andrei arrived early; I arrived on time, cold but full of anticipation in my black skirt, strappy top, white sweater, and red rubber-soled cowboy boots (bought in Romania and great for walking on ice). When Andrei saw me, he said, "WOW! You look gorgeous." I hoped he really meant it. We set off together walking toward the club, Andrei sweetly holding my arm so I would not fall on the ice.

I noticed right away that Lisa had a very generous cleavage. Since she was shorter than me, I stared at her boots to avoid any eye contact with her cleavage.

We spent the evening dancing and getting to know each other (and I noticed that Andrei had all the right moves). As the hour grew later, the club became more crowded. Andrei did not mind the crowds, but he sensed that I did, so we left and walked through the freezing February drizzle toward the old National Theater. Located on the top floor of the theater, Lapataria lui Enache (Milkbar of Enache) was one of Bucharest's best-known music scenes, popular with foreigners and noted for live jazz and an older crowd. We listened to the music and danced a little. And then we kissed.

She kissed me! I felt like, in the entire world, there was only us. We kissed again. The whole room was watching, but I didn't care. For me, time had stopped. It was getting late and I didn't know how to ask Lisa to allow me to accompany her home without her getting the idea that I wanted something more. So I just asked. We took a cab back to the apartment where Lisa was staying, kissed goodnight, and I left.

I walked all the way home singing and dancing in the freezing rain like a crazy Romanian. Several policemen and a few cab drivers even stopped to ask if I needed a ride. I didn't. I was in love. But I wasn't so sure about Lisa, in spite of her apparent affection. When I got home, I was totally exhausted but could not sleep. I wanted to remember every second.

Although I had had a great time, I thought Andrei was "too nice." The following day, I e-mailed a friend who persuaded me to give nice guys a chance.

I had been rejected before for being too nice and if Lisa decided not to go out with me again, I vowed to become a criminal.

Andrei and his father came to Giurgiu the following Tuesday. I had already scheduled a meeting with the president of the County Council, the same gentleman who had gotten me into St. Andrew's. We were kept waiting for an hour and a half (so we knew this was a person of power). When we were finally escorted into the office, we were offered the obligatory coffee, cookies, and small talk. Mr. Cazacu artfully engaged the president with jokes and name-dropping, and the two men verbally strutted around in a who-knew-who competition.

Finally, we got down to business and the reason for our visit. Romanian words were flying all over the room, and I had trouble keeping up. There were times when I thought my cause would prevail; then I would catch a few more words and realize it might not. Phone calls were made and more people summoned, but in the end, we walked away no further along than when we started. Although the president was a powerful man in the county, he was not powerful enough to resolve my problem.

Back at my apartment, I fixed lunch for Andrei and his father. As evening approached, I asked Andrei if he thought his father could get back to Bucharest by himself. At first, Andrei didn't get it so I asked him again. I wasn't thinking about sex (really). I just wanted to spend more time with him. Andrei stayed for three days.

In the end, despite the Cazacu's help, I did not succeed in my effort to establish the volunteer program — at least not at St. Andrew's. I just moved the project to another orphanage in Giurgiu where I was not considered a spy.

21
Growing Up In the Shadow of Ceausescu

As I came to know Andrei, I began to understand something of his family's bitter struggle for survival under a brutal regime. Early on, the Cazacu family had run afoul of the communists. Because they were not members of the communist Party or even sympathizers — sufficient evidence to establish dissident status — the family was frequently targeted for retribution. Over the years, relatives were imprisoned, the family home appropriated, employment and educational opportunities denied, and Andrei arrested and beaten.

This is Andrei's story.

Andrei Dumitru

Born Andrei Dumitru Alexandru in 1939, Andrei's father was raised by an upper-class, French-speaking family in the educated and cosmopolitan city of Bucharest. His father, Nitisor Cazacu, held a prominent position as secretary to the Patriarch of the Romanian Orthodox Church. He was also the parochial priest at Batistei church in Bucharest, but not even a priest could escape the scrutiny of the regime. The unfortunate Father Cazacu was arrested — at least six times — on various trumped-up charges, but he was lucky enough to have a determined wife who called upon the Patriarch to exercise his tenuous influence and succeeded in getting her husband released from prison each time.

When Andrei Dumitru applied for admission to university, there were only 120 spaces available for incoming students. Ninety of these were reserved for members of the communist party. For the remaining 30 slots, there were 900 applicants from the rest of the social classes. In spite of stellar exam results, Andrei Dumitru was not accepted, and was encouraged to try again the following year.

The following year, Andrei Dumitru did indeed try again and this time he was accepted. During his second year, several meetings were held with the covert purpose of exposing class enemies who had "infiltrated the system." At one of the meetings, Andrei remembered a large auditorium filled with students as well as members of the communist Party.

"The first row was packed with secret police all dressed up like workers. The message was that these workers had earned a right to their education, while the rest of us were imposters. One of the students whose name appeared on the informers' list was called to the front of the room where he was publicly accused of his crimes: his mother owned a private business, a pharmacy."

Zoica

Andrei's mother, Zoe (or Zoica), came from a wealthy family in a small, provincial town. After King Michael's abdication in 1947, prosperity turned to misfortune under the oppressive regime of the communists. Suddenly, both families, not yet known to each other, found themselves in the perilous category of "class enemy," in which affluence and education guaranteed membership.

In addition to the obvious attempts to establish control and eliminate dissent (frame-ups, harassment, threats, etc.), the government specified how much money, how many vehicles, and what property an individual could possess. Those with more fortune than allowed by the law were "relieved" of their possessions and/or imprisoned. An impoverished population was much easier to control.

Zoica's family quickly lost most of their material possessions under the new regime. Her father, Gheorghe Marinescu, was imprisoned at the Danube-Black Sea "Death" Canal. Sentenced without trial or conviction, Zoica's father would spend six years doing hard labor at the Canal. During the communist purges, more than 200,000 political prisoners were exterminated during the building of the canal.

After her husband's incarceration, Zoica's mother found work in another town while 14-year-old Zoica was left behind to live with a family friend. Neglected and alone, she could have simply disappeared among the hundreds of thousands of forgotten people. Instead, she chose to learn, earning first prize in every class until she graduated high school.

In due course, Zoica's grandmother and aunt invited her to come to Bucharest to live with them in their tiny one-room flat. Zoica enrolled in high school and in 1958, the summer before her last year of high school, her father was once again sent to prison. One of his colleagues had denounced him for having the courage of a political opinion, and he was arrested as an enemy of the state. This time, Gheorghe Marinescu was incarcerated at the notorious Sighet prison, reserved for the "worst" opponents of the regime — political leaders who supported democratic ideals, academics, religious leaders, and other professionals. Among the prisoners who reportedly visited Sighet were four former prime ministers and seven bishops of the Greek Orthodox and Roman Catholic faiths. In Sighet, the guards were notoriously cruel, torture common, and many did not survive. Today, Sighet is the site of a memorial to the victims of communism.

Because of international protests over human rights abuse, the regime declared a general amnesty in 1964. According to Securitate statistics, more than 10,000 people were released from prison camps. Yet even as the government publicly proclaimed that all political prisoners in Romania had been released, arrests for "conspiring against the regime," or even thinking about it, continued. Zoica's father was released under the general amnesty of 1964.

In an attempt to conceal the family's political status and ameliorate her daughter's file, Zoica's mother obtained a divorce from her father while he was still in prison (they later remarried). This opened the door to the possibility of higher education a tiny bit wider.

After high school, Zoica had the option of attending university or technical school, depending on her political "status" and providing she could meet the requirements for admission. Because of her family's history, Zoica decided to attend a technical school, to which she received a scholarship because of her high test scores. The Communist Party often turned a blind eye if the children of political enemies wanted a nominal education. After graduation, she found work at a medical supply company. Not exactly her dream, but for the moment, jobs trumped dreams.

Meanwhile, for Andrei Dimitru, things were going reasonably well at university. A talented pianist, he served as chief of the Polytechnic orchestra. One of his good friends would eventually become a world-renowned pianist, but Andrei Dumitru would not have the same opportunity. Because of his family's dissident file, the best he could hope for was playing the piano in clubs, so he gave up his dream of becoming a professional musician. He hoped that with an education, he might at least have a chance for gainful employment.

About this time, destiny and a dance brought the two young people together. With her curly brown hair, blue eyes, and winsome smile, Zoica resembled a young Ingrid Bergman in *Casa Blanca*. Andrei Dumitru was smitten. He would be the first man in her life and the only one.

"I met Andrei in his third year of college," Zoica recalled, "and we got married. I had a job, and he went to college"

The next summer, Andrei Dumitru graduated from university with a degree in engineering. Despite his status as a class enemy, he was able to find a job installing radar equipment in planes, and then as an engineer for the state-run phone company.

* * *

From the beginning, Andrei Dumitru knew that Zoica was different. Her miserable life had taught her the value of courage, determination, and independence. Aware of her potential and her desire for higher education, Andrei set out to find a way for her to achieve her dream.

"He encouraged me to pursue my goal," Zoica said, "but it had been six years since I had finished high school, and the system had changed. There were all sorts of things I needed to know in order to pass exams for college that I had not studied in high school. But I was determined, so I studied very hard."

Andrei Dumitru was able to obtain a small loan to pay the obligatory fees, and Zoica passed her entrance exam with ease. She was admitted to university to study physics, finishing her studies with high marks and earning a place in the professional world. But competition in the profession and her desire to have a family convinced her to downgrade her ambition from physicist to teacher.

Finding a job would prove to be almost as difficult as getting into university. "On the day that jobs were to be assigned, Andrei and I waited hopefully in a school corridor for many hours," Zoica recalled. "Finally, I was sent into a room where a list of teaching positions was posted on the wall. Based on my scores in college, I was entitled to pick whichever school I wanted in Bucharest. I wanted to teach in a high school. I expressed my choice, but there was another woman in the room who contested my selection saying that she should get the job because she had belonged to the communist youth organization. They gave her the job."

Zoica's status as the daughter of a political prisoner would continue to influence her life for many years, until the revolution in 1989. She was never allowed the opportunity of full-time employment, only the possibility of a part-time position. Every year it was the same. She would wait anxiously to see if she would have a job. Most years, she was lucky. After the revolution, she finally obtained full-time employment at a local high school.

Andrei Ioan

In 1971, Andrei Ioan Cazacu was born at Caritas Hospital in Bucharest and Andrei Dumitru became "Tata Andrei," or Papa Andrei. By then, Ceausescu's megalomania was in full sway, and the population firmly under his oppressive control. But in spite of the times, the parents were thrilled at the birth of their first child. A second son, Costin Sergiu, was born four years later.

"All my life, I lived in Bucharest, with my parents, in the same house," Andrei recalled. "It was the custom to live with your parents until you married."

More than 100 years earlier, Andrei's great-grandfather had built the family home, a large three-story house on a quiet residential street. Under communism, each family was allowed only one apartment, so the Cazacus were forced to give up the other two floors of their home.

Andrei attended a private kindergarten run by an elderly couple in their home. Lessons were in French, and the school was hidden away from prying eyes. "My family spoke French at home, as was the custom at the time in many middle-class families. But one had to be very careful since speaking French was forbidden by the state."

When Andrei was seven years old, his Uncle Matei defected to Paris where he became an outspoken activist, broadcasting often over Radio Free Europe and BBC News about conditions in Romania. (Today, Matei Cazacu is a renowned doctor in Byzantine history, an expert in the Balkans, and a popular authority on Dracula. He is also a researcher at Centre National de la Recherche Scientifique, teaches at the University of Paris IV, and is the author of 10 books and more than 100 scientific articles.)

In elementary school, Andrei joined the Young Pioneers even though his parents were not members of the Communist Party. In high school, he became a member (mandatory) of the Communist Youth Organization. "There were many ways to build Party membership; indoctrinating the youth was very effective. So I became a happy little communist in my red Pioneer bandana."

For most of his youth, Andrei was hungry and vividly remembers empty shops, bare cupboards, and food rationing, but there was little food to ration. "Our family was entitled to about one loaf of bread a week — if there was any to be had." Only adults with identity cards received the rations, and they would have to be stretched to feed any children. "We would eat off the heel of the loaf as we walked home, which would put a big dent in our week's supply. Bananas and oranges were never seen during those years, except of course, by the corrupt and overfed party officials."

People with relatives or connections in the country could sometimes scrounge eggs, chickens, or vegetables, but most people were slowly starving. Andrei's father knew the butcher and a few other shop owners and thus was able to cadge enough to get by. "At night, my mother would counsel us to 'go to sleep fast and you will not be hungry.'" The family's empty refrigerator sat in the kitchen, silent and unplugged, until 1989.

At home, Andrei's parents avoided talking about the regime or Ceausescu, afraid the children might inadvertently discuss something "criminal" with friends at school, or a teacher might overhear their conversations. As a child, Andrei's mother had been encouraged by her teacher to inform on her parents and friends.

"The secret police had their methods," Tata Andrei recalled. "They had people who would instigate and people who would inform. Their methods worked. Apartment buildings were not soundproof, and everyone could hear everything. Everybody lived close together, so it was very easy to control them — just turn off the water. The people were starving and nobody had time to think about what was going on with the government. Everybody was chasing after food, sometimes for hours a day.

"With the Securitate, it was always a witch hunt. You had to be very careful what you said, and whom you said it to. People disappeared overnight. Children snitched on their parents, wives on their husbands. Everyone lived in fear of everyone else."

Even today, Zoica fears what she does not know. "There is still a horrible connection between what was then and what is now, and people are still afraid that these things could happen again."

A message

One evening during his sixteenth year, Andrei was on his way back to his house after walking his girlfriend home. The night was dark, and when a local police patrol yelled at him to stop, he began to run, unsure who they were because they did not identify themselves. Andrei was a fast runner, but not fast enough. He was quickly caught, thrown into the back of a vehicle, and taken to the local police station. There the police handcuffed him to a radiator, beat him with rubber truncheons, and kicked him in the face with their steel-toed boots. "The communists wanted to send a message to my family."

The next morning, Andrei was released to drag himself home. "Best you say nothing of this," he was told. "And tell your father to keep quiet or your mother and brother will suffer worse."

Like his father, Andrei was passionate about music. "I played the guitar and sang reasonably well, but after the Securitate smashed my fingers, I could no longer play the guitar. And for a long time afterwards, I could not open my mouth or speak."

There would be other messages. Over the years, the family endured harassment and surveillance, their phone was tapped, their mail opened, and they almost lost their home.

147

Meanwhile, Tata Andrei found a position working for the Council of Science & Technology on patents and inventions. Even the government had to turn a blind eye when they needed capable workers. He was eventually fired from this position because of fear that he would reveal state secrets to his brother, the "spy" who had defected to France. During his entire professional career, Tata Andrei was continually thwarted in his attempts to advance his employment. In Romania, everyone had a file, but the government was always more vigilant with dissidents.

Saved by a taxi ride

In the early 1980s, Ceausescu began to destroy central Bucharest to make way for his lavish and ill-conceived civic center. Churches, historic buildings, and homes that had stood for centuries vanished overnight. One freezing night in early spring, Tata Andrei was headed home. There were few taxis on the streets, but somehow he managed to hail one. The driver knew him and said, "Mr. Cazacu, you are my good friend. I will take you wherever you want to go." A man and his pregnant wife were standing close by in the icy rain. Discovering that they lived in the same area, Tata Andrei invited them to share the taxi. The taxi dropped the couple off at their house, but they never paid for their share of the ride.

Sometime later, the government began to bulldoze the houses in the Cazacu neighborhood. Many of these "relocated" citizens were assigned only a single room in the new apartment blocks that were being constructed on top of the ruins of their old homes.

About a year later, Tata Andrei ran into the gentlemen he had shared a cab with on that dreary winter night so many months ago. It turned out that he was one of the chief architects of the "reconstruction" of Bucharest.

"I have never forgotten how you helped me and my wife that night," the gentleman said. "If there's ever anything I can do to thank you ... "

Tata Andrei suddenly understood what it was the man could do for him. "You know, I have this house and they are going to demolish it. Can you do anything about that?"

The architect happened to live on the corner of the Cazacu's street, so at least part of the street would be protected from the demolition. "Maybe you could straighten the street where it curves, and then my house and my neighbor's house would be saved. You can build apartments in front, in back, all around, just make the new street a little straighter and save our house.

"Because of the intervention of this kindly architect, they cut the corner a bit and saved our house," Tata Andrei explained. Today, there are three houses on the street that sit together like a little island, surrounded on all sides by high-rise apartment blocs.

Revolution

When the revolution finally began in December of 1989, 18-year-old Andrei was one of the eager young patriots who helped defend Romania's only television station. On December 22, after a night of intense fighting, the insurgents finally managed to occupy the state-run television station and began broadcasting — live and in real time — the horrifying spectacle of the revolution. The entire country watched spellbound, not quite believing what they were seeing. General Stefan Gusa, then Chief of Staff of the Romanian Armed Forces, was the first man in uniform to appear on TV, announcing that *"armata e cu noi!"* (the army is on our side) and calling on his troops to support the uprising.

By December 24, Bucharest was a city in chaos. Thousands of citizens stormed the streets, eager to be a part of the historical events unfolding hour by bloody hour. Unarmed and unsure who was the enemy, the Revolutionists were quickly challenged by tanks, soldiers, and undercover police. With the military forces now serving on both sides, a fierce and confusing battle raged.

The Romanian flag — with the communist emblem ripped from the middle — appeared on the tops of tanks and on the front of the television station. Bucharest became the site of one of the largest public demonstrations in history, as thousands of jubilant citizens celebrated the end of tyranny.

Andrei recalled his own experience:

From the first hour of the revolution, I knew that history-making changes were at hand, and I wanted to be a part of it. For several days, my family had been glued to the radio, listening in amazed disbelief to reports broadcast by BBC, Voice of America, and Radio Free Europe. Finally, I told my father that I wanted to go — I had to go — and join my countrymen in the fight for freedom. He said "No, that is not the place for you now," and he took my clothes and locked them away. The next day, I went to my mother. She knew there was nothing she could do to stop me, so I hitched a ride to the TV station in a truck with about 20 other patriots. I spent the next few days holed up in a house next to the TV station, helping to keep the broadcasts on the air. This was the first time in decades that Romanians were able to hear (and see) the truth, and it was exhilarating. For three days, I helped load guns and carry food and water to the fighters. I never slept, not one wink. When the fighting finally stopped, I helped load bodies into the backs of trucks: men, women, and children, shot in the head by snipers, crushed by tanks, or caught in the crossfire.

By December 25, the worst was over. For the first time in almost 40 years, Romanians celebrated Christmas Day.

University

Although the revolution had opened a few doors, the new government was still a bipartisan mix of veteran hard-liners and new democrats, and a person's file still weighed heavily on any opportunities they might have. Your file was your social identity: It contained personal information on your background, your parents, grandparents, even your girlfriends and boyfriends. It was your ticket to opportunity, or a guarantee of failure. The Securitate still had a tenuous hold, but it was enough. And because of his dissident history, Andrei's employment and educational options remained limited. Although he applied to the state university, Andrei knew there was no possibility of acceptance. There were only a small number of available slots, and thousands of people were queuing for admission. Private (and expensive) school would be his only alternative. In the fall of 1990, he enrolled at Gheorghe Cristea University Law School, one of the first private universities in Bucharest.

To help pay for his education, Andrei worked at a number of small jobs, the first as a night clerk for one of Romania's first private "convenience" stores. The small, phone-booth-sized shop was open 24 hours a day and sold cigarettes and small grocery items. Andrei was locked in each night when he came to work, and let out again when his shift ended the next morning. This arrangement was designed to prevent him or anyone else from stealing the merchandize. No one trusted anyone, least of all the teenagers.

In the freezing cold, Andrei reported to work each evening. Locked up inside his tiny cell, he shivered through each interminable shift. Whenever he needed to relieve himself, he used a small can inside the shop.

My first night on the job was Easter Eve, and I wept not only because of my own miseries, but also because it was the first holiday I had ever spent away from my family.

After a few months, Andrei was fired with no explanation. "Go home and be happy we do not charge you," they told him. Termination allowed the employer to avoid paying a full salary and to use the employee as a scapegoat for any larceny or pilfering that occurred (often by the owners themselves) during his employment. Theft and corruption were still the cost of doing business.

In 1994, Andrei graduated from law school but quickly realized that practicing law would be impossible under the current government with its communist-inspired legacy of fraud, corruption, and bribery. He would have to be very creative to secure any employment.

In May 1995, Andrei found a position with the Transylvanian Society of Dracula planning and guiding tours in French and English. For the next few years, he found small opportunities here and there. He worked for a while at a manufacturing company, where he was responsible for obtaining the licenses and certifications needed to conduct business in Romania. Although these jobs were hardly commensurate with his education and not particularly rewarding, they did provide a paycheck.

In June 1999, Andrei went to work for the General Union of Manufacturers (Uniunea Generala a Industriasilor) where he honed his nascent marketing and diplomatic skills. Hired to help negotiate contracts for the expansion of Romanian products into Western Europe, Andrei worked with the Economic Mission to Albania to secure partnerships for newly manufactured goods.

Under communism, many private businesses were confiscated. After the revolution, these businesses were returned to their owners. There was a three-year reprieve, during which the government ceased most discriminatory activities. Then the "second wave" of communists returned to power. Because Andrei was not a communist, his employment at UGIR eventually came to an end. The political climate at the time led many Romanians to believe that it was former communist party members who had engineered the revolution.

Meanwhile, Tata Andrei found another job, this time with the Minister of Education in Science. Various government coalitions attempted to convince him to join their cause because he was known to be fair, honest, and a hard worker — much-needed (and rare) qualities in the struggling government. Even the former communist party tried to engage him. "If you are not with us, you are against us." Eventually they became much more direct. "If you don't join our party, we will fire you." That would have been preferable; instead, they suspended him citing vague accusations to establish cause. For over a year, he remained without pay, without the right to rehire, and without the means to retire.

Tata Andrei finally took the only course left to him and went to work for himself, helping Romanians and foreigners navigate the country's convoluted business and commerce regulations. Andrei soon joined his father at Cazacu & Associates, where in the course of building their consulting business, the two Cazacus developed strategic relationships with the French Embassy, various Romanian ministries, and local business leaders.

Andrei was working for his father when he met Lisa in 2003. Although he had not found an opportunity to carve out an independent future for himself, he had found a satisfying niche. Friends and clients sought his advice and valued his opinions. He was respected and appreciated, values he would later miss in America, where his "foreignness" would cause him to be treated like a second-class citizen in more than one employment situation.

Reflections

Throughout every day of his life, Andrei's family was the rock that anchored and sustained him.

My mother never had a toy in her life until my father gave her a doll, which she still treasures. Most of her life was a struggle and it didn't get any easier when my grandmother came to live with us for five years, until her death from senile dementia. Mother taught us to love and respect family above all else, and to care for those in need, even during difficult times.

My father has always been my best friend, encouraging and inspiring me. From birth, my parents taught us to cherish the values of family and justice. My move to America was very difficult for my parents. They wanted me to be happy and I had found a woman I could be happy with. In their mind, I was very brave to immigrate to a new country, 'showing fantastic courage to face life in a foreign land,' but in my mind, I was simply abandoning my family.

Reflecting on the years since the revolution, Mama Zoica said, "There has not been enough change. We are still scared, scared of the people who don't want to change. And the trouble is, we put our hopes in the young people. We were hoping the old generation would die out and the young people would be fair and honest. But the young people only imitate the old; otherwise they cannot be a part of the system. Maybe in the next 50 years, there will be real change."

Today, life in Romania is still difficult for young people. There are few opportunities for productive employment and little chance for a better life. Most people, even doctors, lawyers, and other professionals still earn miserable salaries. Nevertheless, there are small signs of progress.

22
The Tourists

Giurgiu, April 2003
Unlike a year ago when everything was new and the cultural differences so profound, I am now very comfortable in my adopted home. The valleys do not seem so low, nor the mountains so high. There are still things about this country that astonish me, but I cannot complain. Life is good. Meanwhile, two of my dearest friends have decided to get married, and to ensure that I will come home for their weddings, have asked me to be a bridesmaid. I will go home in July for McCandlish's wedding and again in November for Julia's marriage. If I had made the trip home during my first year, I'm not sure I would have returned. But now that I have invested so much of myself in Romania and in the people I serve, I will be back. No question.

Through friends in Giurgiu, I met a couple who had a son born with hydrocephalus, a condition caused by an accumulation of cranial fluid that leads to an enlargement of the head. It is typically treated successfully in Western medical practices with the surgical insertion of a shunt.

When Danut was born, nearly 10 years after the fall of communism, the doctor told his parents that their baby was a monster, that he did not have a brain, and that they should let the child die. This was —

unbelievably — still the conventional wisdom in Romania at the time. Fortunately for little Danut, his parents ignored the advice and took their baby home. Months later in great secrecy, another doctor performed the surgery to install a shunt. By this time, however, the child's head had already grown abnormally large.

When I first met Danut, he was a darling, blue-eyed, happy little boy of six, with a large, cone-shaped head. He was also desperately in need of a new shunt, but because his parents had ignored the counsel of the first doctor, and the second doctor had performed the surgery in secrecy, they were having difficulty securing approvals for another surgery.

Andrei and his father heard about the family's plight and came to Giurgiu to visit them several times. Tata Andrei spent many hours consulting with medical personnel in Bucharest and was eventually able to put the family in touch with a pediatric specialist. He did all of this at his own expense and on his own time, something people in Romania typically do not do. The parents were overwhelmed with gratitude; helping someone and expecting nothing in return was a complete anomaly to them. The community had not been sympathetic to the family's situation. Neighbors had shunned them, believing they must have done something very bad to have a child with such a disability. But because of the caring concern of the Cazacus, a door was opened.

Unfortunately and for various reasons, Danut did not get his new shunt until 2005, and he was never allowed to go to school. The school for the disabled was only for the mentally disabled. In fact, Danut spent most of his short life within the confines of his family's tiny two-bedroom apartment.

Money, or the lack thereof, was also a large part of Danut's problem. Bribery in the medical profession was all too common in Romania in 2003, as it was in most former Soviet countries. I even heard about a doctor who told his patient, "If you don't pay me enough money, you will not get any anesthesia for your operation."

In May of 2007, Danut developed an infection in his shunt, and did not survive.

Questions on the Iraqi war

Romanians were very open about their opinions, especially the U.S. news items they saw on Romanian television. When the Columbia

Space Shuttle disaster happened, everyone — from store clerks to taxi drivers — offered me their deepest sympathies. While the disaster had not affected me personally, Romanians wanted me to know I had their support. Then we were at war with Iraq, and everyone wanted to talk about the war. And I knew that whatever I said would be regarded as the view of most Americans, including the Peace Corps.

Decades of socialism had left their mark, and Romanians seemed to have difficulty seeing another country as a population of individuals with unique ideas, identities, and values that were not always in agreement with the government. Whenever the Iraq situation came up in adult conversations, I simply acknowledged that it was happening. But when I was invited to speak at schools, the kids always asked about the war. I used it as an opportunity to reflect on Romanian history.

Most of the kids were between 13 and 15 years old, too young to remember communism. But they had grown up with soda pop, oranges, bananas, pizza, MTV, HBO, and the Internet — things their parents never had. Whenever the kids asked questions about the war in Iraq, I would tell them about the Iraqi people, how they lived in fear, could not speak freely, could not practice the religion of their choice, could not watch TV programs that were not controlled by Saddam Hussein. If this sounded unfamiliar to them, I would compare the similarities of life in Iraq to what life had been like for their parents under communism.

Mom does Romania

The second week in April, my mother and her friend, Carol, came to visit for 10 days. It was Mom's first trip to Europe. A few days before she left the States, Mom (a nurse) started taking a popular prescription sleep medication. I'm not sure why, but since she had never traveled to Europe and hadn't seen me in a year, I understood that she might have some sleepless nights. Apparently the sleeping pills were not enough, so Mom had mixed things up with some over-the-counter drugs that immediately guaranteed a rocky ride to Romania.

By the time their plane arrived in Amsterdam enroute to Bucharest, Mom had taken so many pills she thought she was having a stroke. Unable to walk, Carol took her to the airport medical facility, where they stabilized her enough to diagnose her condition: She was high on drugs.

"You can't get on a plane like this," the nurse explained patiently. "You're either going to have to go to a hotel or pay a fee to stay here and sleep it off." Carol immediately tried to change their flight, but there was only one flight a day to Bucharest, and Carol did not know how to reach me in Giurgiu. Finally, the nurse told Carol, "If you can get her on the plane, do it." Carol found a wheelchair, got Mom on the plane, and strapped her in. Mom was so high she could have flown to Bucharest without the plane.

I had hitched a ride to the airport with the mayor of Giurgiu, who was traveling to Hungary on business. His Honor had graciously arranged to lend us his car and driver for the return trip to Giurgiu. When Andrei and I walked into the airport, there was Mom, sitting on a chair near the entrance, smiling, drooling, and drinking — one of the six Dr. Pepper's she had brought me from home. I was completely mortified; this would be Andrei's first meeting with her.

I took one look at her and realized something was not right. Carol shot me a look that said there was a story to tell. But the telling would have to wait. Andrei and I took Mom and Carol on a whirlwind tour of Bucharest in the Mayor's car, then we went on to Giurgiu while Andrei remained in Bucharest.

Back at my apartment, Mom immediately asked for her pills. Carol pulled me aside, showed me the pill bottle, and said, "This is what your mom is looking for. She's your mother, you deal with it."

Suddenly it was all quite clear. Angrily, I stormed at my mother, "I'm going to give these pills back to you, but if you take them and you have to go to the hospital, you need to understand that you will not get the same medical treatment here that you would in the U.S. And if your heart stops because you take too many of these, you will die." An exaggeration, perhaps, but I made my point.

Mom took the pills anyway.

Over the next few days, we managed a lightening tour of Romania, visiting palaces, medieval villages, mountain resorts, and Giurgiu, where we had a special audience with the mayor, who excused himself from a meeting to welcome Mom and Carol. We visited "my" orphanage, and I was thrilled that someone from home was able to share some of my Romanian experience.

The trip would not have been complete without a visit to Bran Castle (made famous by Bram Stoker's *Dracula)* and Sighisoara, a UNESCO World Heritage site and reportedly the only still-inhabited medieval citadel in the world. This delightfully preserved Saxon town was also the birthplace of Vlad Tepes, the man known as Dracula.

On the way to Transylvania we stopped in Ploesti and had dinner with my *gazda* family. After one of Dana's delicious meals, we headed back to the train station where we discovered that, because they were working on the tracks, there was no platform. And, without a platform, it was a *long* way from the ground to the train.

The absence of a platform necessitated a complex acrobatic maneuver to board the train, making it especially difficult for my mother, then in her mid-sixties. We had only three minutes to get on the train, so we quickly hustled the luggage aboard and Andrei helped me up. Carol pulled herself onboard, then tried to hoist Mom up. It didn't work. I did my best to encourage her, screaming loudly, "They're going to leave without you!" An elderly but robust Romanian gentlemen who had been watching the spectacle offered to help. He grabbed Mom while Andrei got underneath her and, pushing on her ample bottom, tumbled her onto the train.

After touring the sights in Transylvania, we took the night train to Budapest, where we spent two days in this beautiful city of old-world charm, lush parks, and noble bridges straddling the Danube.

After Budapest, we traveled on for a short visit to Vienna. Arriving there, I was elated to see an Internet Café, a Subway restaurant, and a Starbucks-type coffee shop offering my favorite chai latte. And we hadn't even left the station! I could have remained at the train station and been totally satisfied with my Vienna experience.

The night before Mom and Carol were to go home, we had dinner with Andrei and his family in Bucharest. This would be my first meeting with Andrei's mother. Mom, Carol, and I brought flowers, a lovely arrangement of gladiolas and tulips.

Mama Zoica immediately made us feel at home. With wise blue eyes and soft graying curls, she was warm, intelligent, and very sweet. In her tiny kitchen, she had prepared an amazing Romanian feast of cabbage rolls and polenta, celebrated with plenty of wine and *tuica*, the potent homemade plum brandy that is Romania's national drink. Afterwards, Mama Zoica brought out the family albums and it all seemed quite natural, cozy, and touching.

* * *

Easter is the most important religious holiday in Romania, celebrating the resurrection of Jesus Christ and the renewal of life. Everyone dresses in their best, often wearing national costumes for the solemn midnight service. Romanians traditionally paint their Easter eggs red and decorate them lavishly. Other colors are now used and over the years, this beautiful custom has been transformed into an art form.

I spent the holiday with Andrei and his family, and about 11:30 p.m., on Easter Eve, we walked to the neighborhood church. The courtyard was filled with people and the service inside the church spilled over to the outside. As the priest chanted the Easter story, I was once again reminded that God speaks one language. At the end of the service, the priest took the flame from the Christ candle and shared it with the faithful near the front, the light spreading quickly from one to another. Within a few minutes, the lights from hundreds of candles illuminated the worshippers.

After the service, the streets filled with a twinkling procession of people carrying their lighted candles home, where the festivities would continue with the traditional Easter feast of roast lamb and *Cozonac.*

Back home in Giurgiu, my neighbors presented me with Easter baskets full of the traditional red eggs and real grass, but no chocolate. A friend from home sent me some Peeps, those yummy little marshmallow chicks, which made my holiday just about perfect.

The second Monday after Easter, Romania remembered their dead with a day of commemoration. The cemeteries were bustling, the graves covered with food, homemade wine, and flowers as relatives ate lunch in the company of their dearly departed. If your family had lost a loved one, you bought glasses and ceramic bowls and filled the glasses with flowers and cherries, and the bowls with sweet grains, boiled eggs, a candle, and a wooden spoon, then delivered them to your special friends and neighbors. I remember the kindness of these friends every time I use my bowls.

Labor Day (*Ziua Muncii*) is celebrated in Romania on May 1, and almost everyone goes to the country for a picnic. Andrei and I and several of my Romanian friends crowded into a couple of cars and headed to a park on the Danube River. The park was also considered part of the Romanian frontier and you had to "know someone" to get in. Not only did my friends know the right people, later in the day the Frontier Police joined our outing. Being on duty and in uniform did not deter them from drinking beer (and eating onions to cover it up). As the only American, I was invited to taste every traditional (and nontraditional) food being served. My favorite was *mici,* ground beef and pork sausages seasoned with garlic and spices and served with spicy mustard.

23
Summer Highs

Giurgiu, June 2003

My winter coat was stolen on a train or in a train station sometime during Mom's visit. I had bought the coat on sale at Macy's in New York after searching for weeks for the perfect coat to bring to Romania. It was a Marc Jacobs, so the loss was especially painful. And I have one more winter to survive. Hopefully it will not be as brutal as this one. This time of year, I'm also missing the selection of produce we have in the supermarkets back in the States. We had strawberries for two weeks, cherries for three. Apricots should appear later this month for a week or so. Lettuce is history, but we are starting to see eggplant and green squash.

New best friends

At some point I changed from being "the American on the 11th floor" to being a neighbor and friend, and my nosy neighbors turned out to be my new best friends. Paula, her sister Neli, and their tiny Pekinese (whose name just happened to be Lisa) lived next door to me. I immediately dubbed Paula the "pit bull" because she was unquestionably the best warden I ever had. Paula was the building administrator, and her office was right next to the entrance of our building. Nothing and no one got past Paula unless she determined they could.

Paula, Neli, and I became quite chummy, sharing food and local gossip. I brought them American dishes and they brought me Romanian treats. One afternoon, Paula and Neli brought me a vegetable soup. It was delicious so I asked for the recipe. Neli gave me a list of ingredients and told me to go immediately to the market and purchase them. When I returned home, Neli trotted over and together we made *supa de stevie* (pronounced stav-ee-a). The major ingredient of this zesty soup is the patience herb, but I was never able to find an American version of this leafy green-and-purple thing, which tasted so deliciously sour.

Neli loved teaching me how to do things the Romanian way. I was a willing student and we spent many hours laughing and learning from each other. Once, when it was time to peel carrots, she picked up a knife and I took out my Pampered Chef peeler. She had never seen anything like it. She immediately tried it out and pronounced it a most amazing invention. I bought her one on my next trip to the States.

Keeping cool

Summer in Romania is full of challenges, like staying cool when it is over 100 degrees. I took lots of cold showers and drank gallons of ice tea. Making ice tea was no simple feat since there were no ice trays in Romania, just skinny plastic bags with little pockets that made about 20 small cubes, enough to fill an average-size glass. Romanians would never think of filling a glass with ice. That could be detrimental to your health. They would occasionally put an ice cube or two in their drinks, but most things were consumed at room temperature. I made my Texas-sized tea glass from a plastic bottle.

The thong thing

I've already mentioned the Romanian fondness for see-through blouses and colorful bras. Suddenly, however, the local fashion statement was all about thongs. Walking down any street in Giurgiu, I could immediately tell what color thong underwear most women were wearing. The black thongs worn under white pants were the most obvious, tantalizing and hard to miss. The blue pants with red thongs were, well, interesting. When I asked some twenty-something girls about this practice, they offered no explanation. Just a lot of giggles.

A full refrigerator

A few days after I returned from my trip to the States and McCandlish's wedding, Andrei came down from Bucharest, and I invited some Romanian friends over for a Texas-style dinner. Since I had brought back some special Texas treats, I made chili and queso and mixed up a pitcher of margaritas. For starters, I served up a ranch dip with some veggies. Everything was new to my friends. The evening was fun, the chili a hit, and I shared pictures and memories from my trip home (made all the more interesting by a couple of margaritas).

After everyone left, Andrei and I cleaned up the kitchen and put all the leftovers in the refrigerator. Later in the day, I found Andrei staring into the open fridge. At first I thought he was just cooling down since it was so warm in the apartment. But then he looked at me very seriously and explained what a full refrigerator meant to him. "During communism, there was very little food and no one EVER had a full refrigerator."

I like a full fridge too. But after hearing Andrei's explanation, I realized my reasons were insignificant compared to his. Looking at all the food made Andrei feel safe and secure. I would never be able to comprehend what life had been like for Andrei and his family under communism. I could only work at keeping the fridge full for him.

English spoken here

Summer also gave me a chance to explore other projects. Under the sponsorship of the Mayor's Office, I started two English Clubs with two groups of kids, fifth- through eighth-graders and high schoolers. We met twice a week at the Culture House.

To advertise the club, Andrei and I spent an entire day and many rolls of tape putting up photocopied signs for "free English lessons" on light poles and store windows all over town. The first day of class, I didn't know what to expect but about 20 kids (mostly girls) arrived, full of enthusiasm and anxious to improve their English. Dressed like typical teenagers in jeans and tee shirts, they came from all types of backgrounds. What they had in common was an eagerness to learn, not only English, but also about another culture.

I didn't teach English as such. Instead, we played games and shared fun activities designed to help them improve their conversational English as well as their understanding of American culture. Because Romanian classrooms are very structured and never interactive, the students were not accustomed to getting up and moving around in the classroom. But kids are kids in any culture, so they quickly adapted to this new learning environment. I had a stack of *Cosmopolitan* and *Glamour* magazines that I used for game prizes, and those were highly coveted. Although most young Romanians didn't have much money, they loved parties, movies, music, and pizza, and seemed to value stylish clothes over a full stomach. Over the summer we became friends, exchanging stories about our cultures, our lives, and our hopes for the future.

Media relations

In late June, I began working with a brand-new TV station. The station's reporters were mostly young, inexperienced kids who were thrilled to be learning a trade, but their lack of experience was not an advantage for the station. Since my professional background was marketing and public relations, I offered to help these eager young journalists fine-tune their on-camera reporting. I spent several weeks training the reporters to style their delivery and balance their reporting, and also helped create a marketing plan covering basic market research techniques (market analysis, audience analysis, focus groups, surveys, etc.) the station could implement to broaden their audience and attract advertisers. The best part was that I could watch the results of this project every night on the news broadcast.

Dinner with the ambassador

One evening, Lourrae and I were invited to have dinner with the U.S. Ambassador to Romania, who was in Giurgiu for a meeting. Michael Guest was a kind, intelligent, and comfortable gentleman and over dinner and several bottles of wine, we covered many topics. He had actually been to Corpus Christi (where I had lived for nearly eight years), and his memory of that visit included some of the biggest cockroaches he had ever seen. Not the image I had carried with me from my days in Corpus, but definitely a unique perspective.

A 20-year veteran of the U.S. diplomatic service, Ambassador Guest had served numerous government agencies, including the U.S. Consulate in Hong Kong, the U.S. Embassy in Moscow, the U.S. Embassy in Paris, and as Deputy Chief of Mission at the U.S. Embassy in Prague, where he worked on many of the same issues that were current at the time in Romania. During his tenure, the country established strong alliances with the United States, contributed troops to the war in Iraq, and was admitted to NATO.

When Ambassador Guest, an openly gay man with a long-time partner, arrived in Romania in September of 2001, the practice of homosexuality was illegal. The law was changed shortly thereafter, primarily due to requirements for ascension into the European Union. But Ambassador Guest made sure that this was not an issue during his ambassadorship and let his experience and firm stance against corruption define his service. By the time he ended his Romanian service, he was ranked as one of the most popular political figures in the country.

24
Faith, Hope, Not So Much Charity

Giurgiu, September 2003

   *I continue to have a love/hate relationship with this country.
   From buying grades in school to bribing train conductors,
   operating orphanages, even getting a marriage certificate,
   everyone is on the take. The workers make so little money
   they feel they are entitled. Nevertheless, I have seen small but
   significant changes during my time in Romania. Minimum
   wages (figured in Romania on a monthly basis) have
   increased from $52USD (in 2001) to $82, pensions are up,
   foreign investment continues to rise, and young people are
   optimistic.*

   Often, I inwardly fumed at the blatant corruption, discrimination,
and suspicion of anything new in this country, but I would not allow
myself to become discouraged. Almost always, something unexpected
would happen to renew my hope.
   In late September, my little city in southern Romania marked its 600
years of existence with four days of celebration. Andrei and I saw most
of the concerts from my balcony, but on the evening of the folk music
performance, we decided to brave the crowds. A celebrated Romanian
singer was performing and the square was packed. Towards the end
of the performance, the star invited children from the audience to join
him on stage. One young man lifted his handicapped sister from her

169

wheelchair and carried her up the stairs to join the other children. He was immediately stopped by the officials working the concert and quietly escorted off stage, while the other children raced forward. Somehow the famous singer saw what was happening and invited the two siblings on stage. The little handicapped girl was obviously thrilled as her brother twirled her around. The delight in her face was better than any music and I silently applauded the singer for his bold statement.

Even today, you rarely see handicapped people anywhere in Romania. Many are sent away as small children to orphanages and those who are raised by their families endure ridicule and scorn from society, a burden many parents find difficult to bear. Changing this attitude will take years and many more small steps like the one we witnessed at the concert. A struggling economy, rampant corruption, and lack of a social infrastructure contribute to the difficulties of those suffering from physical or mental disabilities.

Romanian customer service

One afternoon, I made the mistake of washing my cell phone along with the sheets in the washing machine. Although it came out very clean, it no longer worked. I took the phone to a mobile phone shop in town. Florin took my phone apart, cleaned it, dried it, oiled it, and tried to get it to work. When the battery would not charge, he walked me to another store to test the battery. In the end, he repaired my phone and charged me nothing. This was kindness and customer service at its finest. In Romania, this was either a mistake or a miracle.

Earlier in the year, I had taken my phone to the same store for a minor adjustment. Another young man helped me. He fiddled with the phone for three or four minutes, then charged me an exorbitant amount of money, which I paid. I then asked for a receipt. He grunted and said he could not provide one. He had, of course, pocketed the money for himself.

Even in 2003, the words "customer service" had no real significance in Romanian society. In the little dry goods store I frequented (about one-fourth the size of a 7-11 store in the States), there were clerks posted on every aisle. Everyone wore uniforms, in every store, in every business. Despite the extraordinary number of staff and the spiffy uniforms, customers could not expect any special service, nor answers to questions such as where to find something, or whether the store carried a specific product. Under communism, clerks had authority and customers were simply a nuisance. The slow, surly service encountered everywhere seemed to echo the old regime's grand contempt of profit. Low salaries were part of the problem, but the legacy of rudeness and indifference persisted, almost as an entitlement. Evidently many Romanians had not yet grasped the free market paradigm that service and satisfaction = sales = profit.

Learning English — at no extra charge

My English Club at the Culture House was going well. By the end of the summer, I had established a core group of eight high-school girls. Although I called the program an "English Clubs," it was so much more. Besides being a culture-sharing experience, we were forming unique friendships. I was still meeting twice a week with the girls when all of a sudden, the director of the Culture House decided he wanted to charge the girls to attend. I knew this would mean that only those who could afford to pay would come, and this was in total opposition to everything I had worked for as a volunteer. I asked the vice-mayor for help, explaining that this was a service the city was providing to the children and that my services were free. The vice-mayor made a phone call, and the issue was never discussed again.

One day we were playing a game that involved describing various places. I asked the girls to tell me about their bedrooms. Most shared bedrooms with siblings, but one young lady was an only child and had her own. She told me her room was a mess all the time. I explained that, when I was young, my mother would go into my messy room, put everything on my bed, and then clean the room. Before I could go to bed, I had to put everything away. The girls thought this was hilarious and one even shared it with her own mother. She later complained that her mother thought enough of my mom's practice to use it with her own daughter. Even from thousands of miles away, my mom was having an impact on Romanian mothers.

A trip back in time

Romania is full of dichotomies. People still use a horse and cart for transportation, yet Romania is one of the leading markets in Eastern

Europe for information technology. One weekend, I had a chance to experience life in the timeless, tranquil Romanian countryside; I was invited by a co-worker to visit her country home.

On a bright, cloudless fall afternoon, we arrived at her cottage, a two-room, mud-brick house that was probably 100 years old. One of the rooms was a kitchen (more like a food preparation room since there was no sink or stove), and the other was a sort of day room/bedroom. The bed was covered with a thick wool comforter slipped inside a soft cotton duvet, perfect for the chilly weather. A large fireplace opened to the kitchen on one side, and the bedroom/day room on the other.

There was no running water, only a well and a bucket. There was no indoor plumbing, but there was an outhouse. And there was no cook stove, but there was an outdoor wood-burning oven.

During the weekend, we grilled our food, picked ripe apples and quince, breathed the pristine autumn air, and slept like logs. I wondered how hard it would be to live like this every day. I could not imagine how you would cook or keep warm in the winter, or visit the outhouse with three feet of snow on the ground. I couldn't even imagine taking a bath. I am definitely missing the pioneer gene.

All-or-nothing Romanian elections

I take my right to vote seriously. I even voted while I was in Romania. So I watched closely when Romania held an important election in the fall. The vote was on several new amendments to the Romanian constitution, among them abolishing compulsory military service, extending the term of the presidency, and allowing foreigners to own property. The government needed a 50-percent-plus-one vote for a victory. They got that in spades by spending 1 million Euros on advertising (including spots by national celebrities like Nadia Comaneci), car raffles, giving away socks and food to the poor, and having the mayors of several villages stump door-to-door. And when the Romanians voted, the choice was simply YES or NO — all or nothing. Either every amendment passed or no amendment passed.

The town the world forgot

Romania is home to Europe's last leper colony. For decades, few people ever went near the little community of Tichilesti, tucked away among the green hills and lime trees of southeastern Romania, 140 miles from Bucharest. Most knew it only as a refuge for those afflicted with Hansen's disease, commonly known as leprosy.

On the Daily Telegraph Web site in September 2005, Michael Leidig wrote about Tichilesti:

> *Cristache Tatulea, the mayor of the Romanian village of Tichilesti, has a simple test to show visitors how times have changed in his fiefdom: he offers them his hand. "Ah good, you are one of the ones who will shake it," he says, a smile lighting his tanned face. "In the old days, nobody would do that at all. ... "*
>
> *Now, however, decades of near-total isolation and extreme poverty are drawing to an end, largely thanks to a British diplomat who aims to bring the lepers back into society. Jonathan Scheele, the European Union's ambassador to Bucharest, read about the lepers on the Internet and immediately did what no Romanian official had ever done, went to see the colony for himself.*
>
> *"When my Romanian driver found out we were going there, he refused to drive any further and I had to walk through the forest without him," Mr Scheele recalled.*
>
> *"The colony was not what you would expect; it was very calm and peaceful. It was remarkable to talk to people who had spent their entire lives in this compound. They came as teenagers and now they are old. Some married here, had healthy children who grew up and left the colony, and have entered old age without ever leaving."*
>
> *At that time the condition, caused by a bacillus that attacks the skin and nerves leaving limbs and eyes severely disfigured, was still seen by Europeans as a "divine punishment."*
>
> *Romanian lepers suffered even more under the communist dictator Nicolae Ceausescu, who regarded the illness as an affliction of the decadent West. Victims were evicted from their homes, had their possessions burnt and were forbidden to use notes or coins in case they passed on the infection. Tichilesti*

was removed from official maps and many locals still claim to be unaware of its existence.

Today only 23 mostly elderly residents are left, of whom the oldest is 92. Some live in long pavilions, resembling monastic cells, while others, including Mr Tatulea, have built their own houses. There are two churches, one Orthodox, one Baptist, and a farm on which the colony grows corn. Mr Tatulea, 73, also has his own vineyard. His sister-in-law, Ioana Miscov, lost her fingers and feet, and tends her neat house and garden by crawling on her hands and knees. ...

Now more than 70,000 Euros have been allocated to refurbish the crumbling leper colony and supply satellite television and radios to link residents to the outside world. The EU has also funded an information campaign about leprosy. Contrary to popular opinion, it is not highly contagious: infection occurs only after prolonged exposure to droplets from the nose or mouth. Since the 1980s leprosy has been curable, although it remains a problem in parts of the developing world.

Ironically, leprosy does not affect vital organs, so victims often live well into their senior years. Today, multi-drug therapies can cure leprosy in as little as six months. But modern medical treatments have arrived too late for most of the citizens of Tichilesti. While no longer contagious, the residents bear their scars — lost limbs, knobs instead of fingers, stubs for noses, empty eye sockets — with quiet dignity, savoring life and grateful for each new day.

25
Hearts, Diamonds, and Visas

Giurgiu, November 2003
Whenever I'm frustrated or homesick, I find comfort in the
small gifts given to me by special friends back home: blue
birds from Camilla and Gabriel, cool rocks from a trip to
Sedona with Julie, rosary beads from Mischelle, a gold star
from Pat, a pewter heart from Lillian, and all the treasured
pictures and cards that adorn my apartment.

In early November, Andrei had his interview at the U.S. Embassy for his tourist visa, which he would need to go with me to the States for Julia's wedding. Applying for a tourist visa sounds like such a simple task but it can be a very complicated process. First, Andrei had to go to a specific bank and pay the $100 visa fee. To find out what time and date he had been assigned for his interview, he had to access the appropriate Internet site with the PIN they gave him at the bank. His appointment was accordingly scheduled for three weeks from the date he paid the fee.

In the interim, we busied ourselves completing the paperwork, which included a letter of invitation from Julia. Andrei was in a category of people who are typically denied a tourist visa — young, single, male, with no money and no property. Thus, the logic goes, the traveler would have no real reason to return to Romania.

Apparently the law presumes that every visa applicant is a possible immigrant. Therefore, applicants must overcome this assumption by demonstrating that the purpose of their trip to the U.S. is business, pleasure, or medical treatment; that they plan to remain for only a specific, limited time; and that they have a permanent residence outside the U.S. and will return to their home country after their visit. Andrei had previously been granted visas to travel to France on several occasions and had always returned to Romania within the specified time limit. We hoped that this would at least demonstrate his good faith and perhaps tip the scales a bit in our favor.

On a cold, rainy afternoon, we set out for the Embassy. All the way there, I kept hoping the gloomy weather was not an omen of how things would go for us. The embassy was housed in a lovely old historic building with high ceilings, an ornate wood staircase, and splendid adornments. In the consulate section, there was a large waiting room with five windows, similar to those in a bank.

We arrived for our appointment at the designated time, only to discover that a number of other people also had the same appointment time. We waited, along with everyone else, for Andrei's name to be called. While we waited, we heard some interesting stories about why people believed they should be granted a visa. The best story belonged to an attractive (and most entertaining) young man in his mid-twenties who claimed he was with a circus and needed to rejoin his troupe. He spun a wonderful tale of incredible feats, but could not produce any pictures, schedules, or other documentation to prove his claim.

When Andrei's name was finally called, they asked him a few questions, reviewed the paperwork, and told us to come back at 3:00 to pick up his visa — his admission ticket to the U.S. We felt like we had won the lottery, and in a way, we had.

I was in love a million times

Andrei and I had now been dating for almost nine months, and although I was more than fond of him, I wasn't "there" yet. I needed time to let down my guard and feel secure in the relationship. More than once I cautioned him, "Don't even say the words, don't go there, you're getting too serious and you know I'm going back to the States." But despite my protestations, Andrei told me he had already passed first base. I, however, was still in left field. Andrei was in love. I was in like.

As our relationship grew more serious, I prayed, God, if this is meant to be, I need a sign. Andrei was such a wonderful man, but I knew I was going back to the States at the end of my service, and he had made it clear he did not want to go. I did not want to invest too much in a relationship that was destined to fail, and have only a broken heart to take home.

Our first date was on February 22, I was born on November 22, and Andrei was born on August 22. It wasn't exactly Moses' burning bush, but it seemed to me to be more than coincidental. I had my sign.

Andrei:

I had to pass many "tests" to win Lisa's heart: her mother, her gazda, *her friends and co-workers. I had been in love a million times before, but there was a difference between being in love and loving Lisa. And, although I cared deeply for Lisa, I was probably the only crazy Romanian who didn't want to go to America. I was terrified at the prospect of leaving my home for a foreign country I knew nothing about, even though I knew that Lisa had done this unequivocally by coming to Romania. But she always knew she would be going home at the end of her service. In Romania, family is treasured above all else, and I could not imagine leaving my parents, my brother, and my country behind while I followed my heart to America*

The solution to this problem, in my mind, was simple: Lisa would have to stay in Romania. I loved her and love would conquer continents. Or so I hoped.

A proposal

For several weeks, Andrei had been torturing himself with thoughts of having to move to America if we married, considering every possible alternative that might allow him to remain in Romania. I, of course, believed that the only alternative that would allow him to remain behind was death (by my own hand, if he didn't change his thinking). In fact, on the night before we left for Julia's wedding, scared witless of the unknown, Andrei half-heartedly started a quarrel with me, hoping I would either stay in Romania or leave him behind. I was not fooled.

Andrei had never lived outside of Bucharest and although it was an enlightened city for a post-communist country, life in the U.S. would be a complete change for him. Andrei had visited France and Hungary and had seen other lifestyles, but his idea of life in America was very much influenced by what he had seen in American movies and on TV. He truly believed there were drug dealers on every corner and that we all carried guns. As Andrei told me, "American films are violent. I saw things that terrified me."

But as the months went by, Andrei began to realize that he had no life "without Lisa." It would not matter where we lived.

And so, we began to make our wedding plans, blending old customs with our own new traditions. In Romania, engagement rings are not a common practice. Romanians typically buy a plain gold wedding band, which the girl wears on her right hand until the wedding, when it is placed on her left hand. Many young people today do not observe this custom, but if the couple does decide on an engagement ring, they normally choose it together.

Throughout the fall, Andrei and I scoured antique and jewelry stores for the perfect engagement ring, something that would be symbolic of both Romania and my own American traditions. A week before we were to leave for Texas, we went to yet another shop in Bucharest, where we found the perfect ring, an antique white-gold solitaire. The ladies in the shop fussed and gushed over us as I tried on the ring, over and over again. Gushing is not common for store clerks in Romania, and I wasn't sure if this display was because I was an American or because Andrei was so charming. The ring was expensive by Romanian standards, several hundred dollars (later appraised in the U.S. for about $1,000).

Although I now had my beautiful ring, with all its history and symbolism, I still had not received a proposal. Later I would learn that Andrei did not want to propose until he had the ring. Something he had learned from American movies.

Andrei:

On the Saturday before we were to leave for Julia's wedding, Lisa and I planned to eat Chinese (a treat I knew Lisa was looking forward to) and see a movie. I decided to make a slight change to our plans: I would make my marriage proposal that day. I went over the scene in my mind many times, but I had no idea what I was actually going to say. I hoped that the special location I had chosen and my love for Lisa would help me choose the right words.

Finally, the day arrived, bright, sunny, and bitterly cold. When I insisted we get off the subway at Unirii Square, Lisa was immediately puzzled. And when we headed up the big hill toward the Patriarchal Cathedral, Lisa started sputtering, full of questions. "Why did we get off the subway at Unirii? Where are you going? We're going to miss our movie."

The Cathedral had been the center of the Romanian Orthodox faith since 1668, and I had known it since childhood. It seemed the perfect setting for my proposal.

I, of course, could not understand why we had gotten off the subway at Unirii instead of Grozavesti, where the restaurant was, and Andrei offered no explanation. It was freezing as we headed up the hill, and I had no idea why Andrei, at this particular moment in time, even wanted to go to church. I knew that his grandfather had been a priest and secretary to the Patriarch, but I couldn't figure out what that could possibly have to do with Chinese food and a movie.

Inside the church, ancient icons glittered in the incense-filled shadows. The enduring faces of sacred images stared down at us as Andrei led me to the Patriarch's chair, where his grandfather had conducted so many services. I took off my coat and turned to Andrei, who was suddenly on his knee. My heart leapt and I'm sure I stopped breathing for a few seconds. Andrei was the man I had waited for my entire life and for the first time, I was speechless. Gently and with great purpose, Andrei took my hands in his and began to speak the most beautiful words.

"You are the sun of my sky, the stars in my eyes, and the air that I breathe. I know that there will be many waves in our lives, but I want to ride those waves with you." Then he asked me to be his wife. Through a flood of tears, I answered YES! I felt as if the world had stopped and we were the only people in it. Oblivious to our surroundings, we kissed, cried, and embraced.

Suddenly a priest in flowing black robes and a serious head cover came running toward us. "No kissing is allowed in the church, this is a sacred place," he scolded.

"It's okay, Father," Andrei said. "I just proposed."

"Well then, that's all right," he sputtered. He then insisted on giving us a blessing and crossed our foreheads with scared oil. A wrinkled old *buni* in a heavy brown coat and warm Russian hat approached us. She was ecstatic that she had witnessed our special moment and told Andrei what a wise man he was for proposing in a church. And if he proposed in a church, she hoped he would also marry in one.

Afterward, we called Andrei's parents and my mother. Then we went to the Peace Corps office to use their computers to share the news with the rest of my family and friends. *Then* we went out for Chinese and a movie. As planned.

26
Julia's Wedding

Austin, Texas, November 2003
> *Coming from post-communist Romania to modern, frenetic, excessive America, I felt gratitude for my blessings and freedom, as well as a newfound contempt for our extravagances.*

Just before I left the U.S. for Romania, I had arranged a blind date for Julia. During my first year in Romania, the blind date turned into a storybook romance and finally, a marriage proposal. I had hoped the wedding would take place after I returned to the U.S, but since it would not, it gave me a great excuse to travel home. And this time, Andrei would be coming with me, albeit reluctantly. *"Man, in Texas they will shoot me on sight."*

We left for the States on November 20th, and after an exhausting two-day trip, including a night in Amsterdam, we arrived at the airport in Austin. Mom and Julia were a little late coming to meet us. Standing outside the airport in the 80-degree weather with our winter coats in our hands, I asked Andrei about his first impressions of the United States.

"Do the people look different? Are they dressed differently? Do they sound different?" But he simply stood there, oblivious to the people and the surroundings, his eyes on bright beam. What had captured his attention and raised his blood pressure were the cars. "All these cars. The cars of the movies and the cars of my dreams. I am happy here."

Later, Andrei would tell me how impressed he was by all the individual houses (compared to block after block of apartment buildings in Romania). He also observed that life in America was very fast-paced, and that "there are no drug dealers on the street corners and your citizens are not armed."

We would be in Austin for three wonderful weeks of wedding activities, Mexican food, margaritas, Texas barbecue, warm weather, and introducing Andrei to my world.

Welcome to Texas

The evening before Thanksgiving, the groom had his bachelor party and Andrei was invited. Before we left Romania, a Peace Corps Volunteer had told him that in order to see real American culture, he should visit a Hooters restaurant. Andrei took her seriously and was happy to learn that the first part of the bachelor party would take place there. The Hooters folks happily snapped a Polaroid shot of Andrei surrounded by American "culture." He prized this picture like a trophy and showed it to everyone who would look. After Hooters, the guys proceeded to another venue where pictures were not allowed, and the real party began.

We spent Thanksgiving at Julia's parents' home with 75 other people, including the wedding party and Julia's family. It was one of those gorgeous Texas days, with everyone wearing shorts and the backyard filled with all kinds of outdoor activities. Andrei quickly made friends and was the coach of an impromptu soccer game. By the time the day was over, he was hot, sweaty, stuffed with turkey, and utterly content.

Andrei had never been to a wedding in his life. Like everything else in the U.S., Julia's ceremony would be new to him. At the church before the wedding, a gospel band played lively music and the wedding guests were encouraged to join in. Andrei was the first one dancing in the aisle. I, unfortunately, missed his performance because I was getting dressed with the other bridesmaids.

The reception was a typical Texas barbecue with brisket and all the trimmings, even a margarita machine. Andrei became an instant fan of Texas margaritas and no one thought to warn him about the power and punch of tequila. Andrei was never a big drinker; he never even had a drink until he graduated from college. He drank a few beers now and then and shared in the traditional holiday wine and *tuica,* but he was not prepared for tequila. To Andrei, the sweet frozen concoction had a taste and smell that seemed more like a milkshake than a shaker upper. The next morning, he could not figure out what had happened to him, and suffered miserably from his first hangover through the rest of the day. It only takes one time with tequila.

Andrei did, however, clearly remember dancing with "green sweater" at the reception. A wedding guest wearing a green sweater had invited Andrei to dance. She obviously had had a few margaritas and danced like she was at a singles bar. Andrei loved to dance and could move his backside in a delightfully intoxicating way, but even he was taken aback by the woman's suggestive moves and kept glancing at me for some sort of signal as to what he should do. I found the whole situation hilarious; Green Sweater's husband was the biggest guy in the place. I assured Andrei that most Americans did not dance that way, unless tequila was involved.

After the wedding we spent some time with friends, and even went to San Antonio for a day. Mom and I found time to go shopping for a wedding dress, since my own wedding would take place just three short months after our return. We went to an exhausting number of shops and as we dragged ourselves into the last one, I was beginning to think I would have to go back to Romania without a wedding dress. Looking around the small boutique, my heart sank. The prices were much higher than those of the dresses I had looked at earlier. We selected a few dresses and as I was about to try them on, a rack in the back of the store caught my eye. There it was, THE dress, the one with everything I was looking for — simple, elegant, affordable, and it had an empire waist. I walked out of the dressing room and Mom cried, "That's it!"

For me, the highlight of the trip was seeing my hometown through Andrei's eyes. It was like seeing it for the first time.

27
Joy to the World

Giurgiu, December 23, 2003
  *'Tis the season to be jolly. And really cold. This will be
  my second Christmas in Romania and I will not miss all
  the commercialism that is so much a part of the American
  holiday. I am moved that the focus of the holiday here is the
  joy and blessings of the season. It is not about presents or
  decorations; it is about the birth of Christ, good will, peace
  on earth, and great food.*

As Christmas approached, I witnessed the slaughter of several fatted pigs, mostly from the window of the maxi-taxi on my trips to Bucharest. This year, however, I was more prepared for the all-important "specialty" foods the Romanians cherish during their Christmas celebrations. I was quite sure that I would not be eating pig's ear, but I was looking forward to the cabbage rolls.

In October, my English Club girls had asked if they could have a Christmas party for the orphans. Through our work together, the girls had learned that there were orphanages in their very own community. Previously, they had been unaware that orphans were still present in Romania, much less in Giurgiu, and I was pleased that they had come up with the idea on their own.

Quite coincidentally, I had been volunteering at an Austrian-funded orphanage in Giurgiu, which housed about 10 children between the ages of nine and 11. Casa Speranta, or House of Hope, was unique in that it provided an alternative to state institutions by housing the children in a group home with a more family-like environment. When I suggested the party to the staff, they welcomed the idea.

While I was back in the States in November, I had mentioned the girls' party to my friends and family. They responded generously, donating craft supplies, candy, and more than $250 in cash (a lot of money in Romania). We set a budget for the party and the girls would be responsible for purchasing all the gifts, food, and beverages. They would also be accountable for every lei they spent. The girls decided that games would make better gifts than individual toys because they could then go back to the orphanage after the holiday and play them with the children.

On the appointed afternoon, we all trooped over to the orphanage, carrying brightly wrapped packages, oranges and bananas, freshly baked pastries, and sodas — an absolute feast for our little guests of honor. Lourrae came with us, bringing an astonishing supply of beads and craft materials. We played games, made beaded jewelry, decorated crowns, and snacked on party treats.

The afternoon was a great success and the kids were delighted to have these young people in their lives. The local TV station even aired a story, not about the American working with the orphans, but about a girls' club volunteering their time with the kids. It was all about Romanians helping Romanians. Imagine that. But ideas had been planted and were taking root for real relationships and community service. In the process, the girls had learned a valuable life lesson, that giving back is almost always more fulfilling than receiving.

And the gift these girls had given me would last a lifetime.

* * *

I had planned to join Andrei and his family in Bucharest for Christmas, but before I left, the English Club girls and I were going to have our own little Christmas celebration. Most of the girls had never learned to cook and did not help much in the kitchen at home. When I realized this, I knew that I wanted to have a party that would be not only a fun event, but also a learning experience. We would cook some of the party food ourselves as part of the "learning experience," but I was not convinced that any of the food we cooked would turn out as planned.

First, I reviewed the contents of the special cabinet in my kitchen, which contained the most valuable commodity a Peace Corps Volunteer can have: American junk food. I decided to serve food the girls would not be familiar with, such as Oreo cookies and Hidden Valley Ranch dip with fresh vegetables. I knew the "dip" concept was unfamiliar and eating raw vegetables would be equally unique.

I scoured my Peace Corps cookbook for recipes for typical American foods and settled on pancakes and carrot/raisin salad; the salad to introduce raw carrots in a delicious way, and the pancakes since what Romanians call pancakes were really crepes. I wanted them to experience big, fluffy pancakes made the American way, served with the Aunt Jemima syrup I had hidden away in the special cabinet.

The morning of the party I bought all the necessary ingredients as well as a few Romanian goodies in case the American offerings were a flop. I couldn't have a party without American soda pop, so Coke was also on the menu (you can get Coke all over the world and it seemed totally appropriate for our holiday get-together).

The day started off very cold with lots of snow and ice on the ground. Around mid-morning it began to snow again. I didn't think much about this since it seemed to snow all the time lately, but when I looked outside a few hours later, the snow had not stopped. But I had decided that nothing was going to interfere with my party or my trip to Bucharest for Christmas — not even the weather. Little did I know.

Andrei called in the early afternoon to tell me they had started to close the roads. My only thought after his phone call was: I will need to dress warm when I leave for Bucharest.

The girls arrived at my apartment on schedule and started cooking while I supervised all eight of them in my tiny kitchen. The carrot salad was highly praised, the dip was demolished, and the pancakes and syrup were a huge hit. I gave each of the girls a book (in English), tied with a colorful ribbon.

I had been saving all the magazines I had received while in Romania. I used them as teaching tools and shared them with other volunteers, but I still had a stack about three feet high. As Peace Corps Volunteers, we received *Newsweek* every week; the other magazines came either in care packages or via regular forwarded mail. I moved the stack to the middle of the floor and invited the girls to dig in. When all the magazines had been claimed, we pored over them and laughed at the news and gossip, some more than a year old.

About 4:30, Andrei called again to tell me that the road from Giurgiu to Bucharest was now officially closed. I realized that if I was going to make it to Bucharest, I had to get to the train station fast; traveling by maxi-taxi was no longer an option. The girls helped me clean up and I quickly packed, hoping to make the 5:30 train.

At 5:00 p.m. on Christmas Eve, I set out in the frigid dusk, a cold Siberian wind whipping the snow along the streets. The unheated train station was packed with holiday travelers as well as those just trying to get home. Some people were traveling to Bucharest, others to small villages along the way, and about half to the town of Videle. I bought my ticket and was told the train was running about an hour late.

An hour passed. No train. Two hours passed. Still no train. I sat there with my backpack and my big Santa bag filled with gifts in the freezing station and thought about reading, but it was too cold to take off my mittens. I decided to pass the time attempting to converse with some of the other stranded people. At first, it was not obvious that I was not a Romanian. I was completely bundled up and my hat and scarf covered my red hair. But when I started to talk, it became all too apparent. A crowd gathered, and I was the featured attraction. People wanted to know why an American was in Giurgiu, where I worked in Giurgiu, what life was like in the U.S. — all the typical curiosities attached to a (rare) foreigner.

I welcomed these opportunities for cross-cultural exchange, always hoping to change perceptions of volunteerism and what real life was really like in the U.S. They loved that I had a Romanian boyfriend and were surprised that I could speak their language. As usual, someone produced food and it was shared. We all enjoyed the tasty Romanian bread, sausages, and cheese.

Finally another train pulled into the station. An announcement was made that the train was going to Bucharest, and about half the people jostled outside to the platform. We waited, shivering, our breath suspended in the freezing air, for another 30 minutes before we were finally allowed to board the train. After I maneuvered my baggage into the car and settled down on a bench seat (this was a Personal Train, the slowest and cheapest), another change was announced. All Bucharest passengers had to disembark, and all Videle passengers were invited to board the train.

My heart sank as I watched the Videle train leave the station. The Bucharest-bound passengers trudged miserably back into the station, where at least we were out of the snow and wind. I began to realize just how cold I really was. By now it was well past 8:00, and I knew Andrei's family was waiting for me to begin their Christmas celebration. Under normal circumstances, I would have already been toasty warm in Bucharest, enjoying the Cazacu holiday feast. But these were not normal circumstances.

About 9:00, another train came along and the announcement for Bucharest was made once again. We boarded the train and I immediately realized that the entire *inside* of the train was covered with ice and snow. The benches were topped with about three inches of white powder, and the floor was an ice-skating rink. The train had been sitting idle on a spur, obviously with all the windows down. There were about eight of us in this aging icebox on wheels, and we quickly closed all the windows that we could.

By 9:30, we were finally moving and someone started skating down the aisle. I was so cold at this point it even looked like fun. We amused ourselves by taking turns, using the benches to propel ourselves. When the skating ended, we began to talk, about nothing and everything. We were all cold, and we were all going somewhere to be with people we cared about for the holiday. I didn't even know their names but we made an immediate connection. _

When we needed another activity to take our minds off the cold, someone started singing a Romanian Christmas carol. Others joined in. When the group finished singing, they asked if I would sing an American carol. And this was how it went, first a Romanian carol, then an English carol. The cold melted away as the music warmed us with camaraderie and Christmas cheer.

About midnight, the train finally pulled into the Bucharest station. The streets were silent, deserted, and covered with beautiful virgin snow. Public transportation had shut down hours ago and there were no taxis. I was sure we would have to walk miles through freezing snow and ice to Andrei's house, but Andrei had commandeered an illegal cab that was out taking advantage of the stranded. He had brokered a deal with the driver for an exorbitant amount of money to wait with him at the station *until* my train arrived. There was no other option; Andrei knew that if he let this taxi go, he would never find another. So we decided to get our money's worth and offered a ride to a couple of the carolers.

It was nearly 1:00 in the morning when we finally arrived at Andrei's home. The family had waited for me and had not yet eaten dinner, a gesture that touched me deeply. A small but merrily decorated Christmas tree sat on the buffet; Biz, the fatted family cat, rested hopefully beneath. In a corner of the room, a tall, beautifully painted ceramic *soba* tried valiantly to warm the room. The table was set with delicate china from a bygone era, on a traditional lace tablecloth. White lace curtains framed the frosted windows.

We began the celebration by singing traditional Christmas carols, many of which now sounded familiar after my experience on the train. Mama Zoica had made a book of Romanian carols for me, which Andrei and I still use at Christmastime. I had not expected anything from the Cazacus but with what little money they had, they had bought me gifts I would cherish: French perfume, holiday napkins, costume jewelry, a Christmas wreath, and kitchen utensils. We finally sat down to a delicious dinner of cabbage rolls and polenta. I was finally warm — inside and out.

28
Sex in the City

Giurgiu, February 2004

Most of the time when we interact with people, especially those from a different culture, we never really know if we touched them. But I have been given a gift. Every week I witness the effect of friendship and the free exchange of ideas with my English Club girls as they open their minds and hearts to new concepts and new possibilities. They will be my legacy when I leave Romania.

When my English Club girls wanted to know about something, they were not shy. They were curious, persistent, and on a mission. Not long after classes began, they informed me they wanted to learn more about dating, relationships, sex, and birth control. My first reaction was, "You are too young to talk about this," and "Wow, I am so not qualified to talk about his subject."

We set a date eight weeks down the road to give me time to prepare not only a curriculum, but also a psychological approach. I told the girls we could move forward with these classes only if they each had permission from their parents. Every week, I asked the girls if they had spoken with their parents and secured permission to participate in the sex education classes. Each week, they assured me that they had.

The first place I contacted for resources was, or course, the Peace Corps. They offered me a curriculum that addressed this topic, which I would use as a guide. I then contacted Population Services Inc. (PSI), an international organization with an office in Bucharest and, coincidentally, a former Peace Corps Volunteer in its employ. They were a tremendous help, providing me with a complete program along with reference materials, outlines, even games. I sat down and wrote some lesson plans dealing with relationships, the human body, and birth control. As a special bonus, I planned to invite a "secret" guest speaker.

The first two classes were pretty straightforward and fundamental. It was the birth control lesson that would be the most memorable. PSI in Bucharest had agreed to loan me two dildos — one bright purple, the other hot pink — for our demonstrations, along with several packages of condoms. Since I was not planning to go to Bucharest before our class, I called Andrei and asked him if he would go by PSI and pick up a little package for me. Willing to help in whatever way he could, Andrei happily went to PSI and picked up my package. It was not until he was out on the street that he called me. "Do you know what's in this package?" he asked in a panicked, accusatory tone. Of course I knew: educational materials for my English class. Exasperated at my lack of comprehension, he quickly enlightened me. "There are dicks and rubbers in that bag."

In the U.S., we might have been marginally appalled, reasonably excited, or had no opinion what so ever about someone carrying phallic implements around in a paper bag. But this was Romania. They had not yet gone through the sexual revolution. I told Andrei to hold the bag just like he was carrying carrots or turnips on his tram/bus/maxi-taxi ride to Giurgiu.

Finally, the class the girls had been anxiously anticipating and giggling about arrived. The girls had all talked to their parents, of course. Of course not. Hoping this would not become an issue, we proceeded. None of the girls had ever handled a condom before, much less a dildo. We began by opening a few packages of condoms, and the looks on their faces went from totally interested (as in a science project) to totally disgusted. Before the class, I had written down the basic steps for the proper use of a condom and placed them inside blown-up condoms. You don't want to know how I got the blown-up condoms to the class. The girls had to break open the condoms to find the steps, and then put them all in the correct order.

Then the pink and purple dildos were introduced amid much squealing and more giggles. We laughed a lot but in the end, we had taken a serious and important topic — one that is hard for most young people to talk about — and made it easy to understand and less embarrassing. All of this led to frank, open discussions, not only about sex but also about relationships and maturity. I was proud of my girls. They asked all the right questions and participated unabashedly. They were hungry for information, and I hoped that our lessons would help them deal with life's difficult decisions, and make more informed choices down the road.

At the final meeting, I introduced our special guest. The special guest was Andrei. The girls wanted an opportunity to ask questions and get a male perspective on relationships, "the moves," and so much more. Andrei, having been something of a Casanova during his single days, had a lifetime of experience to share. The questions came at him fast, and he responded with a caring honesty that I wish all young women could experience.

* * *

On February 1, Andrei and I filed the paperwork for our Romanian civil marriage ceremony. We planned to be married on Valentine's Day, and the required documentation could only be submitted 14 days prior to the event. Under communism, Romanian family law had followed Soviet customs, largely intended to undermine the authority of religion. Thus, marriage became a function of the state and had to be legalized in a civil ceremony prior to (preferably in lieu of) the traditional church service. In 2004, the government of Romania still recognized only civil marriage ceremonies performed in the Primarie (City Hall). Many Romanian couples however, also choose to hold a religious service in addition to their civil ceremony.

Besides the required Romanian certifications, I also had to provide several documents originally issued in the U.S. These had to be validated with an *apostille* seal, which certifies that a document is a valid copy of an original, and should therefore be recognized as legal in another country.

Here's a partial list of the documents I had to supply:

- Certified copy of my birth certificate (containing the *apostille),* plus a Romanian translation of the birth certificate (obtained from a Romanian notary office)
- Affidavit stating that I was free to marry (obtained from the U.S. Embassy in Bucharest, no appointment necessary)
- Prenuptial Certificate (health certificate)
- Proof of termination of any previous marriages, along with the requisite Romanian translation, even though I had not been married before.

We had already contacted the Marriage Office about the documents we would need, and we thought we were prepared. We were wrong. But we were only off by two documents and several thousand lei in bribes. According to the Romanians, the affidavit I had provided from the U.S. Embassy stating that I was free to marry was not sufficient to prove that I was: a) not currently married, b) not divorced, and c) had never been married. Exactly how you prove you have never been married is still a mystery to me. The officials at the Marriage Office then sent us to a *notar,* a cross between a lawyer and a notary public. The *notar* prepared four pages of information (for a small additional fee), which included where I was born and who my parents were, even though my birth certificate, passport, and Romanian identity card all contained this information.

Then it was back to the Marriage Office, where we were told that the papers they had just sent us to the *notar* to get were not sufficient. We needed an additional paper, documenting the city in which I was born. Never mind that this information was (still) listed on ALL the official documents we had already provided. So it was back to the *notar,* more paperwork, another fee, etc. Then back to the Marriage Office where we were directed to stand in a line to get our form typed. I immediately noticed that there was *one* line and *one* woman who typed all the forms for the entire mayor's office. But we still had 10 days before the ceremony, right?

Next, we needed to select a time for the ceremony. The clerk told us we could get married either very early in the morning or late in the evening, neither of which were good for us. As we debated the situation, the young lady just sat there, oblivious to our concerns. Finally we realized what was going on. She wanted a bribe to give us the time we wanted. After we "bought" a more desirable 1:00 p.m. wedding time, we were finally able to leave.

On the bus back to Giurgiu, a disheveled old man started rambling about being "tired of foreigners taking up space in Romania and doing nothing except making life more miserable for Romanians." He thought I could not understand him because he had heard me speaking English. As politely as I could, a smile plastered on my face, I explained — in Romanian — that I was a volunteer in his country, working with children in orphanages. To be sure he understood, I then defined "volunteer" for him since Romanians had such difficulty understanding the concept. To close the discussion, I added that I was working in his country *fara banii*, without money. He was quiet after that. His wife was embarrassed.

On that day I really hated Romania, even if it had produced the most wonderful man on earth.

29
A Wedding and a Medical Emergency

Bucharest, February 13, 2004
Tomorrow is February 14, Valentine's Day. It is also the day
of my Romanian civil wedding where, surrounded by my new
family in my new culture, I will marry the man I love. And in
five short months, I will marry this wonderful man again in
a church back home in Georgetown. Having two weddings,
each with its special significance, is a nice way to blend our
cultures.

A few weeks before our civil ceremony, Andrei and I visited a
number of shops in our quest for wedding invitations. Romanians do
not typically send out bunches of invitations, and we would be no
different. We settled on 25 elegant ivory cards that included the requisite
information about the ceremony and the reception. We mailed a few, but
most were hand-delivered by either Andrei and me, or Tata Andrei. I
also did something I would never have done in the States: I e-mailed an
invitation to my Peace Corps pals.

Weeks before, I had purchased some lovely white-on-white patterned
Italian material at a fabric store in Bucharest, which I then took to a
tailor in Giurgiu. I described the wedding suit I wanted and within two
weeks, with only three fittings and no pattern, it was done. The suit
was exquisite and fit perfectly. The cost for this custom suit, including

material, lining, and labor, was only about $50 US. God bless my good fortune and my wonderful Romanian seamstress.

The reception would be held at the home of my dear friend, Liz, who had left Peace Corps service and was now the medical officer at the U.S. Embassy in Bucharest. As a diplomat, Liz lived in an elegant apartment in one of Bucharest's more fashionable building. Her spacious home was more like an art gallery than an apartment, filled with Romanian artwork and sculptures, and the perfect place for a wedding reception. Lucky me!

Andrei spent the night before the ceremony at his parent's home. I spent the night at Liz's. When I woke up the next morning, Valentine's Day, I could feel the warm bubble of romance in the air, even though it was well below freezing outside. As I dressed for my wedding, I suddenly longed for my mother and wished she were with me. Liz stepped right in to lift my spirits and loaned me an exquisite string of pearls. Then it was off in a taxi to meet Andrei. I was on my way to wedding number one.

The civil ceremony was held at the mayor's office, an imposing, lemon-yellow turn-of-the-century building with a spectacular glass awning. We were not the only ones getting married that day, and many other wedding parties were lined up in the lobby. We did, however, have the largest number of guests.

Andrei looked very handsome in a gray wedding suit, white shirt, and red tie. When they called "Familia Cazacu," we were escorted into the next room, a surprisingly formal area with a bank of imposing mirrors along the entire length of one wall. The mayor and his staff sat at an elevated table along the opposite wall. An arch of festive red and pink balloons floated behind the table, courtesy of the mayor's office. Our 75 guests (plus their winter coats and goulashes) filled the room.

Because I was a foreigner, Romanian law required that I have an interpreter before the ceremony could begin. Once our interpreter was in place along with our official witnesses, Andrei's brother Costin and his Uncle Matei, who had come from Paris, the ceremony began. If I was nervous before the ceremony, I did not notice it, but I could tell that Andrei was. But once the ceremony began, my knees started shaking.

The five-minute service was conducted by a marriage official who offered a brief explanation of the significance of wedded bliss and then asked the perfunctory questions, Do you take this man to be your husband? Do you take this woman to be your wife? We answered simply *da*.

After we were officially declared married, Andrei and I were taken to the front of the room where we greeted each guest who, in turn, offered us hugs, congratulations, and flowers. By the time each guest had been greeted, the stack of flowers in my arms was nearly over my head. Then as quickly as they had piled up, the guests came and took them from me, one by one. As we were leaving, I saw why. The guests had formed an arch of flowers for us to walk under as we left the mayor's office.

After pictures with our guests, everyone headed to Liz's for the reception. Liz had provided a sumptuous Romanian feast complete with wine, beer, and *tuica*. There was even a Valentine wedding cake. A couple of U.S. diplomats who were Liz's neighbors helped out by serving drinks and picking up plates.

About an hour into the reception, a Romanian priest arrived. He had been mentored by Andrei's grandfather, the priest Nitisor Cazacu, and had come to bless our union. Candles were lit, the blessings were said, and the godparents placed our rings on our right hands, later to be moved to the left in the traditional church ceremony. Since I was not of the Romanian Orthodox faith, the priest was not supposed to do this. He later went to the Patriarch to confess this sin, but when the Patriarch learned a Cazacu was involved, he quickly forgave the priest.

In Romania, the godparents act as advisors to the married couple, who supposedly rely on them for support throughout their marriage. In our case, the godparents, who were close friends and business associates of Tata Andrei, were more of a symbolic gesture.

Green card

We filed the papers for Andrei's immigration visa on February 17. Being granted immigration status results in an automatic green card, subsequently mailed to your U.S. residence. The green card attests to the permanent resident status of an alien living in the United States.

The immigration visa process went much like the application for Andrei's tourist visa, except this time we had to "prove" our relationship with pictures and personal letters from people who were aware of our relationship. The process can be summed up in four words: more paperwork, more fees. Andrei also had to undergo a background check and a medical examination. Since advance assurances that a visa will be issued cannot be provided, applicants are counseled not to make any final travel arrangements, dispose of any property, or quit their jobs until their visa has been issued. Andrei's visa was approved and summarily stamped on his passport without a hassle. The visa would double as a green card until he got his official card in the mail.

La *revedere,* Romania

During my close-of-service physical on March 5, Dr. Dan reexamined the spot on my shoulder that he had noticed a year earlier, declaring that it now appeared suspicious. A specialist was consulted and I was told I needed to return to the States as soon as possible for further diagnosis. No one would say the C word, but it was on everyone's mind.

Because of this, all my well-organized plans for our return to the States changed overnight. I would have to close my service six weeks early to seek medical attention in the States. We made plans to leave Romania on April 4th, and I scheduled a doctor's appointment in Texas for the 7th. I had been derailed by medical problems on the way in; they would now become my exit strategy.

I started saying my good-byes, but it wasn't the same as when I left the States. I knew then that I would see my friends and family again. But many of the people who had become such a part of my life in Romania I would never see again. We would, of course, return to Romania to visit Andrei's family and we would visit some of my Romanian friends, but it would never be the same. These people had made a huge impact on my life, and they were important to me. Leaving made me weep for what had been and for what I would never be a part of again. The vendors in the market, the people at the mayor's office, my English Club girls, the kids at the orphanage, my friends — none of them would ever know how deeply they had affected me.

I also said good-bye to my Peace Corps friends. I had met some remarkable people and had formed very special bonds. They were the only ones who truly understood what we had experienced in Romania.

Later in the week, my English Club was invited to tour the U.S. Embassy in Bucharest. The girls would have an opportunity to see what an embassy actually does and would meet with host-country nationals to learn how Romanians played a role in the day-to-day functions of the embassy. This would be our last meeting.

I was especially sad about leaving these girls. They were all smart, sensitive, and hard-working, with so much potential. But that potential is valid only where people are rewarded for working hard. Romania was not that place, at least not yet. Although I was confident they would achieve much, they had more obstacles to overcome than most. I hoped they knew how much I admired them for accomplishing so much with so little. Perhaps Romania's best hope for the future lies in the new generation of energetic, talented, and optimistic young people, whose dreams may well become reality.

My dear neighbor, Paula, who was my mother, grandmother, warden, advisor, and so much more, gave me a crocheted sweater as a going-away present. I wear it with love, knowing I am forever changed because of her friendship.

The hardest people to leave were Andrei's family. E-mail and phone calls would help bridge the gap, but nothing would replace the daily contact we had with them in Romania.

Leaving Romania was much harder than I thought it would be. There was never any question in my mind that I was anything but temporary, and I thought that knowing this would make leaving easier. It didn't.

I knew that there would be many challenges for Andrei and for me once we returned to the States. We would need to find housing, jobs, and cars, and deal with myriad other details, not the least of which were my health issues. But I had Andrei. We would overcome.

And I couldn't wait to taste Mexican food and real Texas margaritas. Made with limes.

30
Repatriation and Americanization

*Georgetown, Texas, May 2004_*
Andrei and I have slowly begun to adjust to our new life in
Georgetown, and for me, life after Peace Corps, for Andrei,
life in the (not so dangerous) United States. The Peace Corps
tries to prepare you for what to expect when you re-enter life
in the U.S., and I was told that coming home was sometimes
more difficult than adjusting to life abroad. I now understand
why.

Two days after we arrived back in the States, I was seen by a
wonderful doctor who gave us the news that I did have a melanoma on
my shoulder. The confirmation of the news we had dreaded was like
having a piano dropped on your head. Surgery was scheduled for the
following week.

One the day of the surgery, the nurse offered me some Valium to
relax me before the procedure. I declined and asked instead if they could
give some to Andrei and my mother, who were both more nervous than
I was.

Surgery was a happy success, but for such a small area, I ended
up with a sizable scar. The biopsy indicated they had removed all
the cancer and that it had not spread to my lymph nodes. I am now a
walking, talking success story for early detection, but I will have to have

a complete medical exam four times a year for the next two years, then two times annually for the following three years.

* * *

When I arrived in Romania, I had been a starry-eyed recruit and everything had been new and challenging. Living with a host family while training with other volunteers had helped me make a smooth transition into Romanian life. We spent two years working on projects, building relationships, and hoping that we were making a difference. All the while, we had a built-in support network of Peace Corps staff and other volunteers around the country.

But when Peace Corps Volunteers return home, no one has any idea of what you have experienced. I soon realized that most people's tolerance for hearing about Romania was about five minutes. Even Andrei did not totally understand. He was experiencing the same expatriation symptoms as I had experienced when I first arrived in Romania. I did keep in touch with many of my returning Peace Corps friends, and it was nice to talk to those who were having similar issues.

Coming home early put us in an immediate housing crisis but a local developer came to our rescue and made arrangements for us to stay temporarily at a local apartment complex. Two months later, we moved into a wonderful little house in Georgetown that felt like a castle to Andrei.

Legal alien

Andrei was one of the few Romanians who never aspired to move to the United States. In the end, he made the decision to come here so that we could have a better life. And now, after a few months in the U.S., he has begun to understand why people want to live here. He is beginning to live his own American dream.

At first, Andrei missed his family and friends terribly. He missed the lifestyle he had known since birth, where people are less career-oriented and life is more family-focused. "In Romania, people are not defined by where they work. They work because they have to put food on the table. You have doctors socializing with trash collectors, and professional people dining with peasants."

On the positive side, Andrei marvels at drive-through banking, vending machines, garbage disposals, and dishwashers. He adores tuna fish, Mexican food, and margaritas. He cried when he saw the vast selection of vegetables — and beer — in the grocery store. He is not, however, impressed with spinach. "Don't be feeding me any more of that grass." He loves Wal-Mart, where he regularly browses the toy section, listens to CDs, and loses himself amid the astonishing (to him) array of consumer goods.

Unused to our "disposable" society, Andrei saves most things Americans throw away, like empty cans, makeup containers, pill bottles, and toothpaste tubes. *It's a communist thing,"* he explained. And his practice of buying large quantities of bananas, coffee, and meat stems from years of deprivation; he still fears they might not be there tomorrow.

So where do we go from here?

I will always feel blessed that I had the opportunity to be a part of the United States Peace Corps. I will never forget those I served or those I served with. Our bright and cozy home is full of mementos and reminders of our experiences and our blended cultures. Andrei is not yet a citizen. He is a legal alien, meaning he has his green card and can enter the U.S. without a visa.

My English Club girls continue to visit the kids at the orphanage, and I get e-mails from them filled with all the news of Giurgiu. E-mail and phone calls help us keep in touch with Andrei's family and many of our Romanian friends. We treasure their letters and voices and look forward to seeing them again soon.

31
Wedding Bells — Again

Georgetown, Texas, July 2004
We knew when we planned our Romanian civil ceremony that there would also be a second ceremony — a church wedding — in Georgetown. We had our first ceremony in Bucharest so that Andrei's family, our Romanian friends, and my fellow Peace Corps Volunteers could be a part of our union. This ceremony also helped with the immigration process. Andrei could have immigrated on a fiancé visa, but he would not have been allowed to work in the U.S. until after we were married. The Georgetown ceremony will provide an opportunity for my stateside family and friends to meet Andrei and to share our special occasion.

Plans for our July 30th wedding in Georgetown had begun almost seven months earlier when we were in the States for Julia's wedding. Mom, Andrei, and I had visited churches and reception venues, sampled cakes, and talked to caterers, and before we returned to Romania, we managed to select a church and book the reception site, caterer, and cake-maker.

We wanted the church service to reflect the joining of two people as well as two cultures, so we decided to include several Romanian customs in the traditional American service. Instead of having flower girls, we had flag-bearers. Three special little girls carried three special flags — the Romanian flag, the American flag, and the Christian flag — down the aisle. We had no bridesmaids, just "honor attendants." I did not want my friends to have to buy dresses they might not like and would probably never wear again, so I suggested they each buy a dress that would make them feel fabulous. Rather than carry traditional bouquets, each attendant carried a spiritual element of the ceremony, the rings, the Bible, bread and wine, and the Romanian wedding crowns.

Our open-minded pastor allowed us to incorporate some of the Romanian Orthodox liturgy into the Methodist wedding service, including the crown ceremony. After we exchanged our vows and rings, Andrei and I took our first spiritual steps as husband and wife. The crowns were blessed three times "in the name of the Father, the Son, and the Holy Spirit" and placed on our heads. Andrei then led me around the altar three times. According to this beautiful Romanian custom, the crowns symbolize the union of husband and wife with Christ, and their obligation to bear witness to his presence in their lives.

After the ceremony, we traveled in a Model A Ford to a stately Victorian mansion for the reception. The evening was perfect and memorable in so many ways, but it went by too fast. We had about two seconds with each guest and then it was time to cut the cake. Toasts were made and Andrei and I danced to a popular Romanian love song. We did not want the predictable foolishness of tossing the bouquet and garter, so when it was all over, we simply drove away.

Neither of us had eaten anything at the reception so on the way to the bed-and-breakfast, we stopped at a Jack in the Box. I'm sure we looked a little odd — me in my long, white poofy wedding dress and Andrei in his tuxedo. Someone actually asked us if we had just gotten married.

One of our best wedding gifts was the one we gave ourselves. Instead of a wedding day, we had a wedding weekend. We got married on a Friday night, so that we could spend time over the weekend with everyone who had traveled to see us. We had a Mexican rehearsal dinner on Thursday night; a bride's tea, the wedding, and the reception on Friday; and on Saturday, we hosted a pool party and picnic. Saturday night everyone enjoyed a Texas-style barbecue. The weekend ended with a family breakfast on Sunday, and on Monday, we left for our honeymoon in Cozumel. Life was definitely good, and full of promise for the twice-wedded Cazacus.

Epilogue

I have made four trips back to Romania since closing my Peace Corps service. So much has changed, and yet so much has stayed the same. Romania was admitted into the European Union on January 1, 2007. This is a good thing for the country's future, but it has made it difficult for those who suffered the most under communism, the elderly. The poor are still poor, and the rich are still rich. For my in-laws, Tata Andrei and Mama Zoica, their pensions have increased slightly, but their heating bill in the winter is more than their combined pensions. Not only have gas prices increased, so have many other items, such as food, clothing, transportation, and electricity.

There are also more hypermarts (Wal-Mart-type stores), new malls, and even a Starbucks Coffee. More and newer cars are on the roadways, especially in Bucharest. The popular Internet cafes of my service days are now nearly extinct. Most Romanians who use computers now have either DSL or cable Internet at home.

Thanks to membership in the EU, Romania has increased its economic growth and lowered unemployment. But serious challenges still remain, among them improving infrastructure and judicial reform, and eliminating the endemic practices of bribery and corruption. It will be difficult to convince Romanians to seek employment at home. With an estimated 2 million citizens working abroad, there is an increasing shortage of skills in the labor force, and this situation is not likely to change until salaries in Romania increase to at least 50 per cent of what Romanians can earn in other countries.

During my third visit back to Romania, Andrei and I rented a car, something we had never done before. Even though it had been four years since my Peace Corps service, driving in Romania still felt like I was breaking the rules. No driving was ever allowed as a Peace Corps Volunteer. But when I found myself in the midst of Bucharest traffic, I realized I should be happy I never had to drive as a volunteer; the drivers are still crazy and the traffic is still horrendous.

In Giurgiu, the buildings looked the same, but the names on the storefronts had changed, mostly due to the addition of chain stores. In the central part of town, the little office supply store, the bicycle shop, and the locally owned furniture store are gone, replaced by cell phone companies, chain appliance stores, and banks. Three large supermarkets have opened, which is good for lowering prices, but bad for the mom-and-pop stores that had so much character. The open-air market is still the same, with the same wonderful vendors. My fruit and cheese ladies are still in their stalls, remarkably unchanged and as hospitable as ever.

We keep in touch with our friends Mihaela and Cristi, parents of little Danut. It was the first time we had seen them since Danut died in May 2007, and the visit was both joyful and sad, for we missed our little Romanian angel. We learned that his last words had been, inexplicably, "Forgive me."

Paula, the pit bull, is as spirited as ever. Her son and new daughter-in-law, who live with her, had a baby girl this year, so Lisa (the dog) will not be the smallest person in the flat anymore. They also now have air conditioning.

The orphans at Speranta are now mostly teenagers. Five of the original nine kids still live there. One of the young Roma kids was removed from the home by his parents, who took him to Spain where he begs on the street with his family. Another young man is in jail for rape. A third quit school and is working at a restaurant in Austria.

I had not seen the kids in two years, and when I walked into the house, I was immediately embraced by bodies that were definitely adolescent, but still had the hearts of children. The delight in their faces was obvious, and their excitement could be felt all the way back to Texas.

These five boys plus one new little girl are in a better place today than they would have been in the state-run orphanages. But they each still long for a family of their own, even though as teenagers, that dream will never come true for them. It was sad to leave them, and I will always wonder if we really made their lives any better.

We've also visited Dana (my *gazda* while I was in training) and her son, Vlad, in Ploiesti. Vlad is looking at universities now and is a star basketball player in the pre-professional team in Ploiesti. He dreams of coming to the U.S. for college and idolizes Vince Carter of the New Jersey Nets. Dana is doing better than most Romanians. She has totally renovated her apartment and even has a dishwasher.

My English Club is still my proudest achievement as a volunteer. Six of the girls attend universities in Bucharest and all are excelling in their fields. One is studying marketing and public relations, one plans to be a teacher, another is studying architecture, two are pursuing degrees in engineering, and one is already supervising construction sites. After our last dinner together, I received an e-mail from Lavinia (the architecture student). "Lisa, tonight I felt like nothing's changed since I was 17. You haven't changed a bit, and I can't believe how the years have passed. All the memories from the English Club are very fresh in my mind. You meant a lot to us; you definitely changed something in our lives and helped us in growing up. Of course, all my friends know about you and whenever I meet someone new and have to talk about myself, I mention you and the Club."

It is an honor to have known these amazing girls, and it is they who have changed me.

Andrei's brother Costin now lives in Brussels. This has been a great experience for him as well as an opportunity to live on his own, outside of Romania. Andrei's parents still struggle with day-to-day living; a house fire recently destroyed much of the third floor of their home, and their health remains precarious. Tata Andrei still smokes like a chimney, and Mama Zoica remains one of the wisest women on the planet.

Mama Zoica and Tata Andrei came for a visit this year; it was Tata Andrei's second visit, and Mama Zoica's first. Mama Zoica worried that she would not like the food in the U.S. — until she had Mexican food and Texas BBQ. She and Tata Andrei could not get enough of either.

Life with Andrei has been as wonderful as it promised to be. I love being married, and the joy of partnership was totally worth waiting for. We laugh a lot. Food, movies, and his Sony PlayStation are at the top of Andrei's list of things necessary to support life. And I value and appreciate my life in the U.S. much more since my experience in Romania.

Andrei became a U.S citizen in 2007, a journey he never longed for but found to be profound. It was with great sadness and great joy that he took the oath of citizenship. The oath states that "… I absolutely and entirely renounce and abjure all allegiance and fidelity to any foreign prince, potentate, state, or sovereignty of whom or which I have heretofore been a subject or citizen … so help me God." Part of his heart will always be in Romania, but he happily wears a shirt that says, "Romanian American." The 2008 presidential primary provided Andrei with his first opportunity to vote in a U.S. political election. We were both proud.

Andrei and I have enjoyed exploring the U.S. together, most recently to the Grand Canyon and Detroit for the International Auto Show. For Andrei, the car show was the realization of a dream, an opportunity to go live to the "mother" of all car shows.

When I first returned from Peace Corps service, I worked as a PC recruiter for six months before accepting a permanent job with the State of Texas in communications. Since my melanoma surgery in 2004, I have remained cancer-free. I continue to volunteer in various local organizations and was recently a delegate to our county's political convention.

Andrei had a difficult time finding a career path that would not only take advantage of his unique talents and skills, but would also give him a sense of self-worth. He worked in automobile and retail sales for a while, and also as a library assistant and security guard before he finally landed the perfect job. He is now an international flight attendant with Delta Airlines and flies all over the world — truly a dream job for him.

Ironically, just before his interview for the airline position, Andrei did some career testing at a local university, where they discovered that the job for which he was best suited was — international flight attendant. No wonder he loves the job, and the job seems to love him.

Tot este forte bine. Nu ma pot plange. It's all good. I cannot complain.

Peace Corps Today

(Author's note: These statistics were current as of 3/09)

Since its creation in 1961, more than 195,000 Peace Corps Volunteers have served in 139 host countries in every corner of the planet. They've worked as teachers and advisors, helped farmers raise crops, assisted small businesses in marketing their products, and taught women how to care for their infants. In recent years, PCVs have provided education on HIV/AIDS, implemented environmental programs, and helped communities learn computer skills.

Today, more than 8,079 volunteers work in 74 countries, including many that have only recently become nations. Their efforts continue to make a difference, bringing help and hope to generations of people struggling to make a better life.

Some Well-Known Former Peace Corps Volunteers:
Joe Acaba, mission specialist educator astronaut, NASA (Dominican Republic 1994–96)
Ron Arias, senior editor for *People* magazine and author of *The Road to Tamazunchale* (Peru 1963–64)
David Briscoe, chief correspondent of World Desk for Associated Press (Philippines 1966–70)
Dan Carney, reporter for *Business Week* (Benin 1983–85)
Karen DeWitt, producer, abcnews.com (Ethiopia 1966–68)
Thomas Dine, president, Radio Free Europe/Radio Liberty (Philippines 1962–64)

Christopher J. Dodd, U.S. Senator, D-Connecticut (Dominican Republic 1966–68)

Jim Doyle, Governor of Wisconsin, and his wife, Jessica Doyle (Tunisia 1967–69)

Richard "Kinky" Friedman, author of *Blast From the Past* (Malaysia 1967–69)

Samuel Gillespie III, senior vice president, Exxon Mobil Corporation (Kenya 1967–69)

Frank Guzzetta, CEO of Hecht's (India 1968–72)

Robert Haas, chairman of the board, Levi Strauss (Ivory Coast 1964–66)

Taylor Hackford, producer of *Ray, An Officer and a Gentleman*, and *The Devil's Advocate* (Bolivia 1968–69)

Reed Hastings, founder and CEO of Netflix (Swaziland 1983–85)

Peter Hessler, author of *River Town: Two Years on the Yangtze* (China 1996–97)

Joseph W. Lown, mayor of San Angelo, Texas (Bolivia 1999–2001)

Chris Matthews, host of NBC's *Hardball* (Swaziland 1968–70)

Michael McCaskey, chairman of the board, Chicago Bears (Ethiopia 1965–67)

Robert McCormack, executive vice president of Citicorp (Colombia 1968–70)

Carl Pope, executive director of Sierra Club (India 1967–69)

Gordon Radley, president of Lucasfilms Ltd. (Malawi 1968–70)

Donna Shalala, former U.S. Secretary of Health and Human Services, president of the University of Miami (Iran 1962–64)

Paul Theroux, author of *Mosquito Coast* and *Great Railway Bazaar* (Malawi 1963–65)

Acknowledgments

Lisa:

First of all, I am grateful to the Peace Corps for choosing me, and honored to have had the opportunity to represent the United States to the people of Romania.

I also owe a huge debt of gratitude to all the people who sent me care packages. I savored every peanut butter cup, rationed the toilet paper, and made Mexican feasts for my friends. I kept every card and picture sent to me, and hung them on my kitchen door, where they were a constant source of comfort and joy.

I thank Julia Allen Carleton for taking care of my life stateside while I was in Romania. She not only handled my mail, she was also my power of attorney, and I left my life literally in her hands. GX Creative Communications in Georgetown designed and hosted my Web site while I was in Romania, a generosity that allowed me to share my experience with people around the world. Shurgard Storage has my deepest gratitude for storing all my worldly possessions. Also, my appreciation to Allen Rodgers for his help with the *Bread, Salt & Plum Brandy* Web site. But most of all, I will forever be grateful to the people of Romania. Because of them, I will spend the rest of my life with a wonderful, caring, funny, and fabulous Romanian who is the best souvenir ever.

Rosemary:

When I first heard Lisa's story, I was fascinated. I was fortunate to be able to travel to Romania in the process of writing this book, and for me, this effort is all about the amazing Romanian people, and the remarkable gift that is the United States Peace Corps. And, of course, without Lisa and Andrei, there would be no story.

Lisa Fisher Cazacu still views life as a grand adventure and continues to find ways to make it more interesting. She lives in Georgetown, Texas, with her husband, Andrei.

Visit Lisa at www.breadsaltandplumbrandy.com

Rosemary Colgrove has worked as a writer/editor for over 20 years. She has written materials for numerous commercial markets, and published articles in *Austin Home & Living* magazine. Rosemary lives with her husband, Dean, in Georgetown, Texas, and between them, they have five grown children.

- Father, keep us safe
- Lord of Heaven above

- Wrap your arms around us
- Fill us with your love

- Guide us every day
- Hear us when we pray

- Let no harm befall us
- Light the path before us
- Save us when we stray

- Help us be aware
- Of your constant care

- Let your peace surround us
- Let joy fill the air

- Lord, we give you thanks
- We lift holy hands

- Lord of all creation
- Father of all nations
- King of seas and lands

Printed in the United States
143651LV00003B/54/P